TAPAS COOKBOOK

55 Easy Recipes For Cooking Traditional Spanish Food At Home

Emma Yang

© Copyright 2023 by Emma Yang - All rights reserved.

Without the prior written permission of the Publisher, no part of this publication may be stored in a retrieval system, replicated, or transferred in any form or medium, digital, scanning, recording, printing, mechanical, or otherwise, except as permitted under 1976 United States Copyright Act, section 107 or 108. Permission concerns should be directed to the publisher's permission department.
Legal Notice

This book is copyright protected. It is only to be used for personal purposes. Without the author's or publisher's permission, you cannot paraphrase, quote, copy, distribute, sell, or change any part of the information in this book.
Disclaimer Notice

This book is written and published independently. Please keep in mind that the material in this publication is solely for educational and entertaining purposes. All efforts have provided authentic, up-to-date, trustworthy, and comprehensive information. There are no express or implied assurances. The purpose of this book's material is to assist readers in having a better understanding of the subject matter. The activities, information, and exercises are provided solely for self-help information. This book is not intended to replace expert psychologists, legal, financial, or other guidance. If you require counseling, please get in touch with a qualified professional.

By reading this text, the reader accepts that the author will not be held liable for any damages, indirectly or directly, experienced due to the use of the information included herein, particularly, but not limited to, omissions, errors, or inaccuracies. You are accountable for your decisions, actions, and consequences as a reader.

SUMMARY

Introduction	8

Chapter 1: Spanish recipes	10

Paella de marisco
Patatas bravas
Croquetas
Tostadas con tomate y jamón
Gambas al ajillo
Empanadas de atún
Mejillones al vino blanco
Tortilla española
Aceitunas rellenas
Calamares a la romana
Revuelto de setas
Chorizo a la sidra
Pincho moruno
Fried eggplant with honey
Pollo al ajillo
Fried octopus with paprika
Fried cod fish
Gazpacho
Grilled vegetables
Fried pork with garlic
Pimientos de Padrón
Ensalada de bacalao
Queso de cabra con miel
Cazuela de ajo
Huevos rotos
Champiñones al ajillo
Salmorejo
Fabada asturiana
Sopa de lentejas
Pan con tomate

Chapter 2: Valencia 56
Paella valenciana
All i pebre
Esgarraet
Fideuà
Arròs negre

Chapter 3: Madrid 68
Huevos rotos con jamón
Cocido madrileño
Callos a la madrileña
Huevos a la flamenca
Cochinillo al horno

Chapter 4: Murcia 80
Zarangollo
Olla murciana
Huevos rotos con alcachofas
Almejas a la marinera
Caldero del Mar Menor

Chapter 5: Catalonia 92
Canelones
Pulpo a la gallega
Caldereta de pescado
Queso de cabrales
Sopa de ajo

Chapter 6: Desserts 104
Crema Catalana
Chocolate and Churros
Tarta de Queso
Leche Frita
Tarta de Santiago

Conclusions 114

INTRODUCTION

Spanish cuisine is a melting pot of influences shaped by the country's history and geography. Spanish food is diverse and delicious from the seafood-rich coastal regions to the hearty meat and vegetable dishes of the interior. The cuisine is known for its fresh ingredients, bold flavors, and simple preparations.

Spain is home to a wide variety of traditional dishes, many of which have been passed down through generations. One of the most famous Spanish dishes is paella, a rice dish that originated in Valencia and is typically made with chicken, rabbit, and various types of seafood. Another famous dish is tapas, small plates of food that are traditionally served as a snack or appetizer in Spanish bars and restaurants. Popular tapas dishes include tortilla española (Spanish omelette), patatas bravas (spicy fried potatoes), and croquetas (deep-fried balls of meat or fish).

Spain is also known for its cured meats, such as jamón ibérico, a cured ham made from the Iberian pig, and chorizo, a spicy sausage often served as a tapa. The country also boasts a variety of cheeses, including the famous Manchego, a sheep's milk cheese that is often served as a tapa.

Spain is also famous for its wines and ciders, produced in regions across the country. Spain is home to some of the world's finest wines and ciders from the Rioja region in the north to the Jerez region in the south.

Spain's Mediterranean climate and coastal regions also provide an abundance of fresh seafood, which is a staple in the country's cuisine. Dishes such as grilled sardines, octopus with paprika, and salt cod salad are all popular seafood dishes in Spain.

In addition to traditional dishes, Spanish cuisine has been heavily influenced by other cultures, particularly those of the Moors and the Jews. Dishes such as gazpacho, a cold soup that originated in Andalusia, and huevos rotos, fried eggs served over a bed of potatoes, both have their roots in these cultures.

Spain is also known for its desserts, which are often sweet and simple. Flan, a creamy custard dessert, is a popular choice, as is churros, a fried dough pastry that is often served with hot chocolate.

In conclusion, Spanish cuisine is a delicious blend of influences, shaped by the country's history and geography. From paella to tapas, cured meats to seafood, the country's food is diverse and delicious and is sure to delight any food lover.

CHAPTER 1

SPANISH RECIPES

Spanish cuisine is known for its rich flavors, bold seasonings, and use of fresh, locally-sourced ingredients. One of the most popular and beloved aspects of Spanish food is the tradition of tapas - small plates of food that are typically served in bars and restaurants.

The origins of tapas can be traced back to the medieval taverns of Spain, where small plates of food were served alongside drinks as a way to keep patrons from getting too drunk. Today, tapas have evolved into a cultural institution in Spain, with an endless variety of dishes to choose from. Some popular tapas include:

- Patatas bravas: fried potatoes with a spicy tomato sauce
- Croquetas: fried balls of meat or fish and vegetables, often served with aioli
- Tortilla española: a traditional Spanish omelette made with potatoes and onions
- Gazpacho: a cold soup made of tomatoes, cucumbers, and peppers
- Calamares: fried squid, often served with a garlicky aioli
- Paella: a traditional rice dish that can be made with a variety of meats, seafood, and vegetables

One of the best things about tapas is that it's a great way to try a variety of different dishes. Many bars and restaurants in Spain offer a "tapa of the day" that changes each day, allowing customers to try new and exciting dishes. Additionally, tapas are often served in small, manageable portions, making them perfect for sharing with a group of friends or family.

Another great aspect of tapas is that it is typically served in a casual, relaxed setting. Tapas bars are often lively and bustling, with patrons standing at the bar or sitting at small tables to enjoy their food and drinks. This creates a fun and sociable atmosphere, making it a great way to spend an evening with friends.

In summary, Spanish tapas are a beloved tradition of small plates of food that are usually served in bars and restaurants. It's a great way to try a variety of different dishes, perfect for sharing with friends, and often served in a casual, relaxed setting. From the traditional dishes like Patatas bravas or Croquetas to the more modern options like Paella or Churros, there's something for everyone to enjoy in Spanish tapas.

Did you know that...

1. Spain is the largest producer of olive oil in the world. The country has more than 300 million olive trees, with most of them being grown in the Andalusia region. Spanish olive oil is known for its intense, fruity flavor and is used in many traditional dishes.
2. Spain is also one of the world's leading producers of wine, with famous regions such as Rioja and Ribera del Duero. Sherry, a fortified wine from the Andalusia region, is also a traditional drink that is enjoyed in Spain.
3. Paella, a traditional rice dish, originated in Valencia and is named after the pan it is cooked in. The original version of paella was made with rabbit, chicken, and snails and cooked over an open fire. Today, there are many variations of paella, with seafood and vegetarian options available.
4. Churros, a fried dough pastry, are often served as a breakfast dish in Spain. They are traditionally served with a chocolate dipping sauce, but can also be topped with sugar and cinnamon.
5. Spain has a long history of preserving food, which is why it is famous for its charcuterie. Spanish cured meats such as jamón ibérico and chorizo are known for their rich, intense flavor and are often served as tapas.
6. Spain is also known for its seafood, particularly its anchovies and sardines. These small fish are often served marinated, grilled, or in a traditional dish such as boquerones en vinagre.
7. Gazpacho, a cold soup made of tomatoes, cucumbers, and peppers, is a popular dish in Spain during the summer months. It is typically served chilled, making it a refreshing dish to enjoy on a hot day.
8. Spain has a long history of conserving fruits, vegetables, and meats with sweet and sour flavors. This is why you can find dishes like Escalivada, a dish of roasted vegetables with olive oil and vinegar, and also many sweet and sour stews like "Cocido Madrileño"
9. Spain has a number of regional cuisines, each with their own unique dishes and specialties. For example, the Basque Country is known for its pintxos (tapas on bread), Catalonia for its use of saffron, and Galicia for its seafood dishes.
10. Spain is also home to the Michelin-starred restaurants, with many of the best chefs in the world. The Spanish cuisine is considered one of the top in the world and has a lot of influence and impact on the culinary industry.

Paella de marisco

Paella is a traditional Spanish rice dish that originated in Valencia, Spain. Paella de marisco, or seafood paella, is a variation of the dish that includes a variety of seafood such as shrimp, squid, and mussels. Paella de marisco is typically cooked in a large, shallow pan over an open flame, and is often served as a main course for special occasions.

 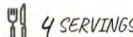 4 SERVINGS 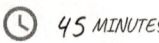 45 MINUTES 500 KCAL MED

INGREDIENTS

- 1 cup of short-grain Spanish rice
- 2 cups of seafood stock
- 1 onion, diced
- 2 cloves of garlic, minced
- 2 tomatoes, diced
- 1/2 teaspoon of saffron
- 1/2 teaspoon of smoked paprika
- Salt and pepper to taste
- 1/4 cup of olive oil
- 1/2 pound of shrimp, peeled and deveined
- 1/2 pound of squid, cleaned and sliced
- 1/2 pound of mussels, cleaned and debearded
- 1/2 cup of peas
- 2 lemons, cut into wedges
- Fresh parsley for garnish (optional)

DIRECTIONS

1. Heat the olive oil in a large paella pan over medium heat. Add the diced onion, garlic, and sauté until softened, about 5 minutes.
2. Add the diced tomatoes, saffron, smoked paprika, salt and pepper and cook for another 5 minutes, stirring occasionally. The smoked paprika will give it a nice smoky flavor and a beautiful red color.
3. Add the rice and stir to coat the rice in the tomato mixture. Cook for 2-3 minutes or until the rice turns translucent. This is the most important step in making a good paella, as it's where the rice gets toasted and absorbs all the flavors of the dish.
4. Pour in the seafood stock and bring to a boil. Reduce the heat to low and let it simmer for about 15 minutes or until the rice is cooked through and the liquid is absorbed. Paella should be cooked over low heat so that the rice is cooked evenly and the liquid is absorbed slowly.
5. Add the shrimp, squid, and mussels to the pan and give it a good stir. Cover the pan and let it cook for about 8-10 minutes or until the seafood is cooked through. The seafood should be added towards the end of the cooking process, as it cooks quickly and can become rubbery if overcooked.
6. Lastly, add in the peas and give it a good stir. Cover the pan and let it cook for about 2-3 minutes or until the peas are cooked through. The peas are added as a final touch, giving the paella a nice freshness and a pop of color.
7. Once the paella is cooked, turn off the heat and let it sit for a few minutes before serving. This will allow the flavors to meld together and the rice to finish cooking.
8. Serve the paella with a lemon wedge and garnish with fresh parsley if desired. Enjoy your delicious seafood paella!

Patatas Bravas

Patatas Bravas, also known as spicy fried potatoes, is a popular Spanish tapa that has become a staple in tapas bars across Spain. The dish is believed to have originated in Madrid in the 1950s and has since become a beloved classic. It is made by deep-frying chunks of potato until golden brown and crispy and then serving them with a spicy tomato sauce.

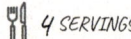 4 SERVINGS   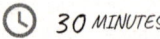 30 MINUTES   300 KCAL   EASY

INGREDIENTS

- 4 large russet potatoes
- Oil for frying
- Salt

For the sauce:
- 1 can of diced tomatoes
- 1 large onion, finely chopped
- 3 cloves of garlic, minced
- 2 tbsp olive oil
- 2 tsp smoked paprika
- 1 tsp cayenne pepper
- Salt and pepper to taste

DIRECTIONS

1. Start by preparing the potatoes. Peel and dice them into 1-inch cubes. Rinse them in cold water and pat dry thoroughly. This step is essential for ensuring that the potatoes are crispy when fried.
2. Heat oil for frying in a deep fryer or a large pot over medium-high heat. Once the oil reaches 350F, carefully add the potatoes and fry for 8-10 minutes, or until golden brown and crispy. Use a slotted spoon to remove the potatoes from the oil and drain on paper towels. Sprinkle with salt while still hot. Pro tip: ensure that the oil is hot enough before adding the potatoes, this will ensure that they cook evenly and will prevent them from absorbing too much oil.
3. While the potatoes are frying, prepare the sauce. Heat the olive oil in a pan over medium heat. Add the onion and garlic and sauté until softened. This should take about 5 minutes. The onions should be translucent and the garlic should be fragrant.
4. Add the diced tomatoes, smoked paprika, cayenne pepper, salt and pepper to the pan. Stir everything together and bring the sauce to a simmer. Let it cook for 10-15 minutes, or until the sauce thickens. Pro tip: stir occasionally to prevent the sauce

Croquetas

Croquetas are a classic Spanish dish made of a creamy filling (usually made with ham, chicken or cod) that is breaded and deep-fried. They are a popular tapa (small dish) and are often served as a starter or snack. The origins of croquetas can be traced back to medieval Europe, where they were made with leftover meat and breadcrumbs.

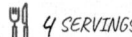 4 SERVINGS   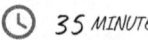 35 MINUTES   200 KCAL   HARD

INGREDIENTS

- 2 cups of cooked and shredded chicken or ham
- 1 cup of all-purpose flour
- 2 cups of milk
- 1 small onion, finely diced
- 2 cloves of garlic, minced
- 2 tablespoons of butter
- 1/2 cup of breadcrumbs
- 1/2 cup of grated parmesan cheese
- Salt and pepper to taste
- Oil for frying

DIRECTIONS

1. Begin by making the béchamel sauce: In a medium saucepan, melt the butter over medium heat. Add the diced onion and minced garlic, and cook until softened, about 5 minutes.
2. Stir in the flour, and continue to cook for another 2-3 minutes. Gradually pour in the milk, stirring constantly, to make a smooth and thick béchamel sauce. Season with salt and pepper.
3. Remove the pan from the heat and stir in the cooked chicken or ham, and grated parmesan cheese. Mix well and let the mixture cool.
4. Once the mixture is cooled, shape it into small croquettes (about the size of a ping-pong ball)
5. Place the breadcrumbs in a shallow dish. Roll the croquettes in the breadcrumbs, pressing them gently to adhere.
6. Heat the oil in a deep fryer or a large pot to 350F. Carefully add the croquettes and fry for about 3-4 minutes or until golden brown. Use a slotted spoon to remove the croquetas from the oil and drain on paper towels.
7. Serve the croquetas hot with a side of your choice, such as a garlic aioli or a tomato sauce.

Tostadas con tomate y jamón

Tostadas con Tomate y Jamón is a traditional Spanish breakfast dish made of toasted bread with a topping of ripe tomato, olive oil, and cured ham. This dish is a staple in Spanish cuisine and is often served with coffee or hot chocolate. It's a simple and delicious dish that can be enjoyed at any time of the day.

 4 SERVINGS  15 MINUTES   300 KCAL   EASY

INGREDIENTS

- 4 slices of crusty bread
- 1 ripe tomato, diced
- 4 slices of cured ham (Serrano or Iberico)
- 2 cloves of garlic, minced
- 1/4 cup of olive oil
- Salt and pepper to taste
- Fresh parsley for garnish
- Directions:

DIRECTIONS

1. Start by preheating your toaster or broiler. Toasting the bread is an essential step in this recipe, as it not only adds a nice crunch but also helps to absorb the flavors of the toppings. To achieve the perfect toasted bread, place the slices in the toaster or under the broiler and keep a close eye on them, as they can burn quickly. Once they are golden brown and crispy, remove them from the heat and set them aside.
2. In a small bowl, mix together the diced tomato, minced garlic, olive oil, salt and pepper. The tomatoes should be ripe and juicy to give the tostadas a nice sweetness and balance out the saltiness of the cured ham. The garlic and olive oil will add a nice depth of flavor and richness to the dish.
3. Spread the tomato mixture over the toasted bread slices. Be generous with the topping, but make sure not to overload the tostadas, as the bread will become soggy.
4. Top with a slice of cured ham, and return the toasts to the toaster or broiler for a minute or so, just until the ham is warm. The cured ham will add a nice salty and savory flavor to the dish and also give it a nice texture contrast.
5. Serve the tostadas hot and garnish with fresh parsley. The parsley will add a nice freshness and color to the dish.
6. Enjoy your Tostadas con Tomate y Jamón with a cup of coffee or hot chocolate. The tostadas are best enjoyed hot and fresh, but they can also be made in advance and reheated in the oven or toaster.

Gambas al ajillo

Gambas al Ajillo is a classic Spanish dish made of succulent shrimp sautéed in garlic, olive oil, and white wine. This dish is a popular tapa (small dish) and is often served as a starter or snack. It is a simple dish that is packed with flavor and can be served with bread to soak up the delicious garlic and wine sauce.

  4 SERVINGS    25 MINUTES   300 KCAL   EASY

INGREDIENTS

- 1 pound of raw shrimp, peeled and deveined
- 6 cloves of garlic, minced
- 1/2 cup of olive oil
- 1/4 cup of white wine
- 1 teaspoon of smoked paprika
- 1 teaspoon of dried oregano
- Salt and pepper to taste
- Fresh parsley for garnish

DIRECTIONS

1. Begin by heating the olive oil in a large skillet over medium heat. Add the minced garlic and sauté for 1-2 minutes or until fragrant.
2. Add the smoked paprika and dried oregano to the skillet and stir for another minute.
3. Add the shrimp to the skillet and sauté for 2-3 minutes per side or until pink and cooked through.
4. Carefully pour in the white wine, and continue to cook for an additional 2-3 minutes or until the wine is reduced by half.
5. Season with salt and pepper to taste, and remove the skillet from the heat.
6. Serve the Gambas al Ajillo hot, garnished with fresh parsley and a side of bread to soak up the delicious garlic and wine sauce.

Empanadas de atún

Empanadas are a popular dish in many Latin American countries, and the tuna empanadas are no exception. These turnovers are filled with a savory tuna filling and can be served as a appetizer or a main dish. They are typically made with wheat flour dough and fried or baked. The history of empanadas can be traced back to medieval Europe, where they were made with meat, fish or vegetables and were considered as a way of using leftovers.

 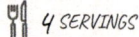 4 SERVINGS 45 MINUTES 250 KCAL MED

INGREDIENTS

- 2 cups all-purpose flour
- 1/2 tsp salt
- 1/4 cup vegetable oil
- 1/2 cup warm water
- 1 can of tuna in oil, drained
- 1/2 cup diced onion
- 2 cloves of garlic, minced
- 1/4 cup diced green bell pepper
- 1/4 cup diced red bell pepper
- 1/4 cup diced olives
- 1/4 cup raisins
- 1/4 cup chopped cilantro
- Salt and pepper, to taste
- 1 egg, beaten (for egg wash)

DIRECTIONS

1. In a large mixing bowl, combine the flour and salt.
2. Slowly pour in the vegetable oil and mix with a fork until the mixture resembles coarse crumbs.
3. Gradually add the warm water and mix until a dough forms.
4. Knead the dough for about 5 minutes until it becomes smooth and elastic.
5. Place the dough in a bowl, cover with plastic wrap and let it rest for 30 minutes.
6. In a skillet, sauté the onion, garlic, green and red bell peppers over medium heat until they are softened.
7. Add the tuna, olives, raisins, cilantro, salt and pepper and stir until the filling is well mixed.
8. Preheat the oven to 375F.
9. Roll out the dough on a floured surface to about 1/8 inch thickness.
10. Cut circles out of the dough using a round cookie cutter or a glass.
11. Place about 1 tablespoon of the tuna filling on one half of each circle.
12. Fold the dough over the filling to create a semi-circle shape.
13. Use a fork to press the edges of the dough together and seal the empanadas.
14. Brush the empanadas with the beaten egg for egg wash.
15. Place the empanadas on a baking sheet lined with parchment paper and bake for 20-25 minutes or until golden brown.
16. Serve the empanadas warm and enjoy!

Mejillones al vino blanco

Mejillones al vino blanco is a classic Spanish dish that features mussels cooked in a flavorful white wine sauce. This dish is a staple in many Spanish restaurants and is often served as a tapa (appetizer) or as a main course. The dish is said to have originated in the coastal regions of Spain, where mussels are abundant and wine is a staple ingredient in cooking.

 4 SERVINGS    20 MINUTES   200 KCAL   EASY

INGREDIENTS

- 1 pound of mussels, cleaned and debearded
- 1 cup of dry white wine
- 1/2 cup of chopped onions
- 2 cloves of garlic, minced
- 1/4 cup of olive oil
- 1/4 cup of chopped parsley
- 1/4 teaspoon of black pepper

DIRECTIONS

1. Start by prepping your ingredients. Clean and debeard the mussels, chop the onions and garlic, and measure out the white wine, olive oil, and parsley.
2. In a large pot, heat the olive oil over medium heat. Add the onions and garlic, and sauté them until they are softened and fragrant, about 3-5 minutes. The aroma of the garlic and onions sautéing in the oil will fill your kitchen and get your taste buds excited for what's to come.
3. Pour in the white wine, add the black pepper and bring to a simmer. As the wine simmers, it will start to reduce and thicken, creating a flavorful and aromatic base for the mussels.
4. Add the mussels to the pot, cover and cook for 5-7 minutes or until the mussels have opened. Discard any mussels that do not open. As the mussels cook, they will release their own juices and the flavors of the wine, onions, and garlic will infuse into the mussels, creating a deliciously tender and flavorful dish.
5. Once the mussels are cooked, remove from heat and sprinkle with chopped parsley. The parsley will add a fresh, herby taste that perfectly complements the rich, savory flavors of the mussels and wine sauce.
6. Serve the mussels in the pot, and enjoy the delicious white wine sauce. Be sure to ladle some of the sauce over the mussels and enjoy it with some crusty bread to mop up all the delicious sauce. The bread will absorb all the flavors and make the dish even more delicious.

Tortilla española

Spanish Omelette, also known as Tortilla Española, is a traditional dish from Spain that is typically made with potatoes, onions and eggs. It is a staple dish in Spanish cuisine and can be enjoyed as a main course or as a tapa (appetizer). Its origins can be traced back to the 18th century when it was a simple and affordable dish that could be made with easily accessible ingredients.

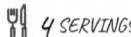 4 SERVINGS   40 MINUTES   300 KCAL   EASY

INGREDIENTS

- 6 large potatoes, peeled and thinly sliced
- 1 large onion, thinly sliced
- Salt and pepper, to taste
- Olive oil for frying
- 6 large eggs

DIRECTIONS

1. In a large skillet, heat a generous amount of olive oil over medium heat.
2. Add the sliced potatoes and onions, and season with salt and pepper.
3. Cook the potatoes and onions, stirring occasionally, until they are tender and golden brown, about 20-25 minutes.
4. Remove the potatoes and onions from the skillet and drain on a paper towel-lined plate.
5. In a large mixing bowl, beat the eggs and then add the potatoes and onions, stirring well to combine.
6. In the same skillet, add a small amount of olive oil over medium-low heat.
7. Pour the egg and potato mixture into the skillet and cook until the bottom is golden brown and set, about 8-10 minutes.
8. Carefully place a plate over the skillet and then flip it over to release the tortilla onto the plate.
9. Add a small amount of oil to the skillet and slide the tortilla back into the skillet, uncooked side down.
10. Cook for an additional 5-7 minutes, or until the other side is golden brown and set.
11. Remove from the skillet and let cool for a few minutes before slicing and serving. Enjoy!

Aceitunas rellenas

Aceitunas Rellenas is a popular appetizer dish in Spain that features olives that have been stuffed with various ingredients. The olives are typically stuffed with a mixture of meat or fish, and sometimes with cheese or herbs. This dish is a staple in many Spanish restaurants and is often served as a tapa (appetizer) or as a party snack. The dish is said to have originated in the Mediterranean region, where olives are abundant and are often used in cooking.

4 SERVINGS | 30 MINUTES | 200 KCAL | MED

INGREDIENTS

- 1 cup of green olives, pitted
- 1/4 cup of minced meat (chicken, pork or beef)
- 2 cloves of garlic, minced
- 1/4 cup of breadcrumbs
- 1/4 cup of chopped parsley
- 2 tablespoons of olive oil
- 1/4 teaspoon of black pepper
- 1/4 teaspoon of paprika

DIRECTIONS

1. Start by prepping your ingredients. Pit the olives, mince the meat, garlic, and parsley, and measure out the breadcrumbs, olive oil, black pepper and paprika.
2. In a pan, heat the olive oil over medium heat. Add the minced meat and garlic and cook until the meat is browned and cooked through, about 5-7 minutes.
3. Remove the pan from heat and let it cool for a few minutes. Once cooled, add the breadcrumbs, parsley, black pepper and paprika. Mix everything together until well combined.
4. Take a small spoonful of the meat mixture and stuff it inside the olives. Press the meat mixture firmly into the olives so that it holds together.
5. Once all the olives are stuffed, place them in a dish and refrigerate for at least 30 minutes to an hour to allow the flavors to meld together.
6. Once chilled, the olives are ready to be served. They can be served cold or at room temperature and best enjoyed with a cold glass of beer or a chilled glass of white wine.

Calamares a la romana

Calamares a la romana, also known as fried squid, is a popular Spanish dish that is typically served as a tapa or starter. The dish originates from the coastal regions of Spain, where fresh squid is abundant. The dish is made by coating squid rings in a seasoned flour mixture before deep-frying them until crispy. The result is a delicious and satisfying dish that is perfect for sharing with friends and family.

4 SERVINGS | **30 MINUTES** | **300 KCAL** | **EASY**

INGREDIENTS

- 1 lb. of cleaned squid
- 2 cups of all-purpose flour
- 1 tsp. of paprika
- 1 tsp. of salt
- 1 tsp. of pepper
- 2 cups of vegetable oil for frying
- Lemon wedges for garnish

DIRECTIONS

1. In a large mixing bowl, combine the flour, salt, and pepper.
2. In a separate bowl, beat the eggs.
3. Place the breadcrumbs in a shallow dish.
4. Dip each squid ring first in the flour mixture, then in the beaten eggs, and finally in the breadcrumbs. Make sure the rings are well coated in each step.
5. Heat the oil in a deep-fryer or a large pot to 350 degrees F (175 degrees C).
6. Carefully add the coated squid rings to the hot oil and fry for 2-3 minutes, or until golden brown.
7. Remove the calamares from the oil and place them on a plate lined with paper towels to drain off any excess oil.
8. Serve the calamares hot, with a side of lemon wedges and a sprinkle of salt, and enjoy the delicious, crispy, and juicy Roman-style squid!

Revuelto de setas

Revuelto de Setas, also known as setas al ajillo or setas revueltas, is a traditional Spanish dish that combines the earthy and meaty flavors of mushrooms with the rich and creamy texture of eggs. This dish is a great way to enjoy seasonal mushrooms and can be served as a breakfast, brunch or as a side dish.

4 SERVINGS   *15 MINUTES*   *200 KCAL*   *EASY*

INGREDIENTS

- 1 pound of mixed mushrooms, sliced (such as shiitake, cremini, and portobello)
- 4 cloves of garlic, minced
- 4 large eggs
- 1/4 cup of heavy cream
- 1/4 cup of grated Parmesan cheese
- 2 tablespoons of olive oil
- Salt and pepper to taste
- Fresh parsley or chives for garnish (optional)

DIRECTIONS

1. Heat the olive oil in a large skillet over medium-high heat. Add the minced garlic and sauté until fragrant, about 30 seconds.
2. Add the sliced mushrooms to the skillet and sauté until they release their moisture and are tender. Make sure to stir occasionally to ensure even cooking. The mushrooms will start to shrink and brown, and will give off an incredible aroma.
3. In a separate bowl, whisk together the eggs, cream, and Parmesan cheese until well combined. Season with salt and pepper to taste.
4. Reduce the heat to medium-low and pour the egg mixture into the skillet with the mushrooms. Stir gently until the eggs are set but still creamy. This should only take a minute or two.
5. Serve the revuelto de setas in individual plates, garnished with some fresh parsley or chives if desired.

This dish can be enjoyed by itself or served with some crusty bread to make a more complete meal. It's a great way to use the mushrooms you have in your pantry, you can use any kind of mushrooms you have available, you can try with wild mushrooms if you want to add an extra touch of flavor.

Note: Keep in mind that the key for this dish is to use good quality mushrooms, as they are the main ingredient and will greatly affect the final flavor. You can also add some bacon or chorizo for a non-vegetarian version.

Chorizo a la sidra

Chorizo a la Sidra is a traditional dish from Asturias, a region in northern Spain. It's a hearty and flavorful dish that combines the spicy and smoky flavors of chorizo with the tangy and acidic notes of cider, the local apple-based drink.

 4 SERVINGS   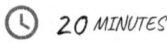 20 MINUTES   400 KCAL   EASY

INGREDIENTS

- 1 pound of chorizo, sliced
- 2 cups of sidra (cider)
- 2 cloves of garlic, minced
- 1 onion, diced
- 1 teaspoon of smoked paprika
- Salt and pepper to taste

DIRECTIONS

1. Start by heating some oil in a large skillet or casserole over medium heat. Once the oil is hot, add the diced onion and minced garlic and cook until they are softened and translucent. This will add a nice sweetness and depth of flavor to the dish.
2. Next, add the sliced chorizo to the skillet. As the chorizo cooks, it will release its oils and start to brown and crisp up. Stir occasionally to ensure even cooking. The smoky and spicy flavors of the chorizo will start to fill your kitchen with a delicious aroma.
3. Once the chorizo is browned and crispy, add the teaspoon of smoked paprika and stir to combine. The paprika will add a nice smoky depth of flavor and a beautiful red color to the dish.
4. Now it's time to add the star of the show: the sidra. Slowly pour in the 2 cups of cider, being careful as it may splatter. Stir everything to combine and bring the mixture to a simmer. Let it cook for about 10 minutes, or until the cider has reduced and thickened slightly. The acidity of the cider will balance out the richness of the chorizo and create a delicious and tangy sauce.
5. Season with salt and pepper to taste. Keep in mind that chorizo is already quite salty, so you may not need to add much.
6. The dish is now ready to be served! Enjoy it hot with some crusty bread to mop up the delicious sauce. This dish is perfect for a hearty meal with a side of mashed or roasted potatoes, or as a tapa to share with friends and family.

Optional: If you want to take it to the next level, you can add some sautéed diced potatoes to the skillet with the chorizo and cook them together for about 10 minutes before adding the sidra. This will give you a more complete dish and add some extra texture and heartiness.

Pincho moruno

Pincho Moruno is a popular dish in Spain, particularly in the southern regions, where it is often served as a tapa in bars and taverns. The dish is a blend of Spanish and Moroccan flavors, and it's typically made with a marinade of spices, citrus, and olive oil. The skewers can be made with different kinds of meat such as chicken, pork, or beef, or even with vegetables like peppers, onions, and mushrooms.

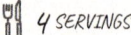 4 SERVINGS   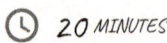 20 MINUTES   250 KCAL   EASY

INGREDIENTS

- 1 pound of chicken breast, pork loin, or beef sirloin, cut into small cubes
- 1/4 cup of olive oil
- 2 cloves of garlic, minced
- 2 tablespoons of paprika
- 1 tablespoon of cumin
- 1 teaspoon of ground coriander
- 1/2 teaspoon of ground cinnamon
- 1/4 teaspoon of cayenne pepper (optional)
- Juice of 1 lemon
- Salt and pepper to taste
- Skewers (if using wooden skewers, soak them in water for at least 30 minutes before using)

DIRECTIONS

1. In a large bowl, mix together the olive oil, minced garlic, paprika, cumin, coriander, cinnamon, cayenne pepper (if using), lemon juice, salt and pepper.
2. Add the meat cubes to the bowl, and toss to coat them well in the marinade. Cover the bowl and refrigerate for at least 1 hour or up to 24 hours to allow the meat to marinate and absorb the flavors.
3. Preheat a grill or grill pan over medium-high heat. Thread the meat cubes onto skewers.
4. Grill the skewers, turning occasionally, until they are cooked through and browned on all sides. This should take about 8-10 minutes, depending on the size of the meat cubes.
5. Serve the skewers hot, garnished with some fresh herbs or lemon wedges if desired.

These skewers are perfect for a summer barbecue or as a tapa in a casual get-together with friends and family. You can serve them with a side of couscous or a simple salad for a more complete meal.

Note: Keep in mind that you can use different kind of meats or vegetables and adapt the recipe according to your preferences. You can also adjust the spices to suit your taste. The key is to marinade the skewers for enough time to allow the flavors to develop.

Fried eggplant with honey

Fried Eggplant with Honey is a simple yet delicious dish that combines the creamy texture of eggplant with the sweet and tangy flavor of honey. This dish is commonly found in Mediterranean and Middle Eastern cuisine, and it's a great way to use up eggplants that are in season.

 4 SERVINGS   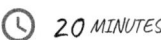 20 MINUTES   200 KCAL   EASY

INGREDIENTS

- 2 medium eggplants, sliced
- 1/2 cup of all-purpose flour
- 2 large eggs, beaten
- 1/2 cup of breadcrumbs
- 1/4 cup of olive oil
- 1/4 cup of honey
- Salt and pepper to taste
- Fresh parsley or mint for garnish (optional)

DIRECTIONS

1. In a shallow dish, mix together the flour, salt and pepper. In another shallow dish, beat the eggs. And in a third shallow dish, mix together the breadcrumbs.
2. Heat the olive oil in a large skillet over medium heat.
3. Dip each eggplant slice in the flour mixture, then in the beaten eggs, and finally in the breadcrumbs, pressing the breadcrumbs onto the eggplant to adhere.
4. Place the breaded eggplant slices in the hot oil and cook for about 2-3 minutes per side, or until golden brown. Drain on a paper towel-lined plate.
5. Once all of the eggplant slices are cooked, heat the honey in a small saucepan over low heat until it becomes runny.
6. Place the fried eggplant slices on a plate and drizzle the honey over them. Garnish with fresh parsley or mint if desired.

This dish can be served as a side dish or as a vegetarian main course. It's a great way to use up eggplants that are in season and a perfect dish to enjoy with a side of rice or a simple salad.

Note: Keep in mind that you can use different kind of flour and breadcrumbs to suit your preferences. You can also adjust the amount of honey to your liking and you can add some spices like cumin, coriander, or cinnamon to the breadcrumbs mixture for a more flavorful dish.

Pollo al ajillo

Pollo al Ajillo is a traditional Spanish dish that is characterized by its simplicity and intense garlic flavor. The dish is typically made by sautéing chicken in a skillet with garlic, olive oil, and white wine. It is a staple in Spanish cuisine and can be found in many tapas bars and restaurants throughout the country.

4 SERVINGS   20 MINUTES   300 KCAL   EASY

INGREDIENTS

- 4 boneless and skinless chicken thighs or breasts
- 8 cloves of garlic, thinly sliced
- 1/4 cup of olive oil
- 1/4 cup of dry white wine
- Salt and pepper to taste
- Fresh parsley or thyme for garnish (optional)

DIRECTIONS

1. Heat the olive oil in a large skillet over medium heat. Add the thinly sliced garlic and sauté until it's fragrant and lightly golden brown, be careful not to burn it.
2. Add the chicken to the skillet and season with salt and pepper. Cook the chicken until it's browned on both sides, about 5-6 minutes per side.
3. Once the chicken is browned, pour in the white wine, and bring the mixture to a simmer. Cook for a couple of minutes, or until the wine has reduced by half.
4. Reduce the heat to low and cover the skillet. Simmer the chicken for about 10-15 minutes, or until it's cooked through. Stir occasionally and baste the chicken with the garlic and wine sauce.
5. Once the chicken is cooked, remove the skillet from the heat. You can serve it hot with a sprinkle of fresh parsley or thyme on top for some added color and flavor.

This dish can be enjoyed as a main course with a side of mashed or roasted potatoes, or as a tapa with some crusty bread. It's a simple and flavorful dish that can be prepared in a short amount of time and it's perfect for a weeknight dinner.

Note: You can adjust the amount of garlic to suit your taste. You can also add some sliced mushrooms to the skillet with the chicken and garlic for a more complete dish.

Fried octopus with paprika

Fried Octopus with Paprika is a classic dish that is common in Mediterranean and Spanish cuisine. The dish is typically made by marinating octopus in a mixture of olive oil, lemon juice, garlic, and smoked paprika before frying. The result is a tender and flavorful octopus that is crispy on the outside and juicy on the inside.

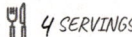 4 SERVINGS   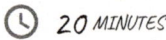 20 MINUTES   300 KCAL   EASY

INGREDIENTS

- 1 pound of octopus, cleaned and cut into small pieces
- 1/4 cup of olive oil
- 2 cloves of garlic, minced
- 2 tablespoons of smoked paprika
- Juice of 1 lemon
- Salt and pepper to taste
- Flour for dusting
- Olive oil for frying

DIRECTIONS

1. In a large bowl, mix together the olive oil, minced garlic, smoked paprika, lemon juice, salt, and pepper. This mixture will be your marinade, it's packed with flavor and will give your octopus a delicious smoky and slightly tangy taste.
2. Once you have your marinade ready, add the octopus to the bowl and toss it to coat it well with the marinade. Make sure every piece of octopus is well coated and has the chance to absorb all the flavors. Cover the bowl and refrigerate for at least 1 hour or up to 24 hours. This time allows the octopus to marinate and absorb all the flavors, it's essential for a tender and flavorful dish.
3. Once the octopus has marinated, remove it from the marinade and dust it with some flour. The flour will help to create a crispy texture and it will also help the octopus to absorb less oil while frying.
4. Heat some olive oil in a large skillet over medium-high heat. We recommend using a skillet with high sides, this will make it easier to handle the octopus and it will also prevent oil from splattering.
5. Once the oil is hot, carefully add the octopus to the skillet. Be careful not to overcrowd the skillet, fry the octopus in batches if necessary.
6. Fry the octopus for about 5-6 minutes, or until it's crispy and browned on all sides. The octopus should have a beautiful golden color and a crispy texture.
7. Once the octopus is cooked, remove it from the skillet and drain it on a paper towel-lined plate. This will help to remove any excess oil and it will also help to keep the octopus crispy.
8. Serve the fried octopus hot, garnished with some fresh herbs or lemon wedges if desired. It's a perfect dish for a weeknight dinner and it's also great as a tapa.

Fried cod fish

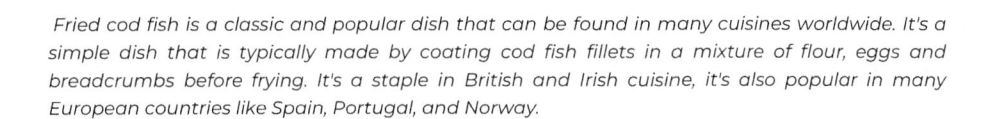

Fried cod fish is a classic and popular dish that can be found in many cuisines worldwide. It's a simple dish that is typically made by coating cod fish fillets in a mixture of flour, eggs and breadcrumbs before frying. It's a staple in British and Irish cuisine, it's also popular in many European countries like Spain, Portugal, and Norway.

4 SERVINGS | **20 MINUTES** | **300 KCAL** | **EASY**

INGREDIENTS

- 4 cod fish fillets
- 1/2 cup of all-purpose flour
- 2 large eggs, beaten
- 1/2 cup of breadcrumbs
- 1/4 cup of olive oil or vegetable oil
- Salt and pepper to taste
- Lemon wedges for garnish (optional)

DIRECTIONS

1. Season the cod fish fillets with salt and pepper.
2. In a shallow dish, mix together the flour. In another shallow dish, beat the eggs. And in a third shallow dish, mix together the breadcrumbs.
3. Heat the oil in a large skillet over medium heat.
4. Dip each cod fish fillet in the flour mixture, then in the beaten eggs, and finally in the breadcrumbs, pressing the breadcrumbs onto the fish to adhere.
5. Once the oil is hot, gently place the breaded fish fillets into the skillet and cook for about 2-3 minutes per side, or until golden brown and crispy.
6. Carefully remove the fish from the skillet and drain on a paper towel-lined plate.
7. Serve the fried cod fish hot with some lemon wedges on the side for garnish.

This dish can be served as a main course with a side of mashed or roasted potatoes and vegetables. It's a perfect dish for a weeknight dinner and it's very easy to make.

Note: Keep in mind that you can use different kind of flour and breadcrumbs to suit your preferences. You can also add some spices like paprika, cumin, or coriander to the flour mixture for a more flavorful dish.

Gazpacho

Gazpacho is a chilled soup that is commonly served in the summertime in Spain, it's a traditional Andalusian soup and it's made of raw vegetables and served cold. This dish is a great way to take advantage of the fresh produce in the summer and it's a refreshing and light soup. Gazpacho is a perfect soup to cool down and energize during hot summer days.

4 SERVINGS   **30 MINUTES**   **100 KCAL**   **EASY**

INGREDIENTS

- 3 tomatoes, peeled and chopped
- 1 cucumber, peeled and chopped
- 1 red pepper, seeded and chopped
- 1 small onion, chopped
- 2 cloves of garlic, minced
- 2 cups of tomato juice
- 1/4 cup of olive oil
- 2 tablespoons of red wine vinegar
- Salt and pepper to taste
- Croutons for garnish (optional)

DIRECTIONS

1. Start by preparing the vegetables, peel and chop the tomatoes, cucumber, red pepper, and onion. Peel and mince the garlic.
2. Place the chopped vegetables in a blender or food processor, add the tomato juice, olive oil, red wine vinegar, salt, and pepper. Blend until smooth.
3. Taste the soup and adjust the seasoning as needed. It should be well-seasoned and have a good balance of acidity and sweetness.
4. Cover the blender or food processor and refrigerate the gazpacho for at least 2 hours or overnight. This will allow the flavors to develop and meld together.
5. Before serving, strain the gazpacho through a fine mesh strainer to remove any remaining chunks of vegetables.
6. Serve the gazpacho chilled, garnished with some croutons or diced vegetables if desired.

This dish is perfect for a summer lunch or dinner, it's light and refreshing and it's also a great way to use up summer produce

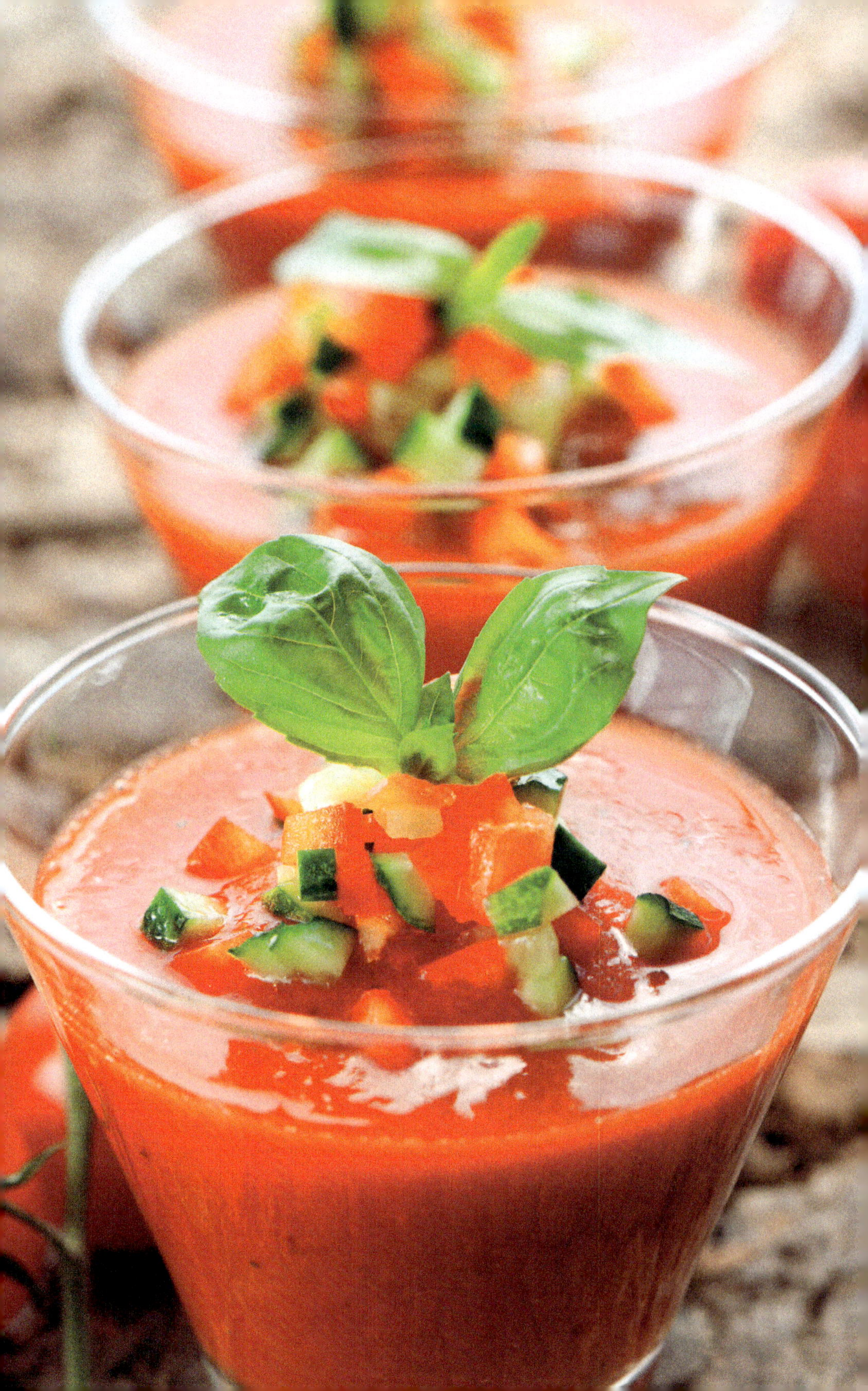

Grilled vegetables

Grilled vegetables are a classic and versatile dish that can be enjoyed year-round. It's a simple dish that's perfect for a summer BBQ or a weeknight dinner. Grilled vegetables are a great way to take advantage of the fresh produce in the summer and they can be easily customized to suit your taste.

4 SERVINGS | **20 MINUTES** | **100 KCAL** | **EASY**

INGREDIENTS

- 2 bell peppers, sliced
- 1 onion, sliced
- 1 zucchini, sliced
- 1 eggplant, sliced
- 1 portobello mushroom, sliced
- 1/4 cup of olive oil
- 2 cloves of garlic, minced
- Salt and pepper to taste

DIRECTIONS

1. Start by preparing the vegetables, slice the bell peppers, onion, zucchini, eggplant, and portobello mushroom. Peel and mince the garlic. Slicing the vegetables in a similar size will ensure that they cook evenly.
2. In a large bowl, mix together the olive oil, minced garlic, salt, and pepper. This mixture will be your marinade, it's packed with flavor and it will give your vegetables a delicious taste.
3. Add the sliced vegetables to the bowl and toss to coat well with the marinade. Make sure every piece of vegetable is well coated and has the chance to absorb all the flavors. Let the vegetables marinate for at least 15 minutes, this will help them to absorb the flavors and to be more tender once grilled.
4. Heat a grill or grill pan over medium-high heat. If you're using a grill, make sure that the grates are clean and oiled to prevent the vegetables from sticking.
5. Once the grill is hot, place the vegetables on the grill, and cook for about 4-5 minutes per side, or until they are tender and charred in places. Keep an eye on the vegetables as they cook, they should have a beautiful char and be tender but not mushy.
6. Remove the vegetables from the grill and place them on a platter. You can also place them on a plate and squeeze some lemon juice over them to enhance the flavor.
7. Serve the grilled vegetables hot as a side dish or as a main course. They can also be served cold as a salad.

Fried pork with garlic

Fried pork with garlic is a classic and popular dish that can be found in many cuisines worldwide. It's a simple dish that is typically made by marinating pork in a mixture of soy sauce, sugar, and garlic before frying. It's a staple in Asian cuisine, particularly in Chinese and Korean cuisine. It's a perfect dish for a weeknight dinner and it's very easy to make.

4 SERVINGS **20 MINUTES** **300 KCAL** **EASY**

INGREDIENTS

- 1 pound of pork loin, thinly sliced
- 1/4 cup of soy sauce
- 2 tablespoons of sugar
- 2 cloves of garlic, minced
- 2 tablespoons of vegetable oil
- Salt and pepper to taste
- Green onions for garnish (optional)

DIRECTIONS

1. In a large bowl, mix together the soy sauce, sugar, minced garlic, salt, and pepper. This mixture will be your marinade, it's packed with flavor and it will give your pork a delicious savory and slightly sweet taste.
2. Once you have your marinade ready, add the thinly sliced pork to the bowl and toss it to coat it well with the marinade. Make sure every piece of pork is well coated and has the chance to absorb all the flavors. Cover the bowl and refrigerate for at least 1 hour or up to 24 hours. This time allows the pork to marinate and absorb all the flavors, it's essential for a flavorful and tender dish.
3. Heat the oil in a large skillet over medium-high heat. A skillet with high sides will make it easier to handle the pork and it will also prevent oil from splattering.
4. Once the oil is hot, carefully add the marinated pork to the skillet. Be careful not to overcrowd the skillet, fry the pork in batches if necessary.
5. Fry the pork for about 2-3 minutes per side, or until it's browned and cooked through. The pork should have a beautiful golden color and be cooked through.
6. Remove the pork from the skillet and drain it on a paper towel-lined plate. This will help to remove any excess oil and it will also help to keep the pork crispy.
7. Serve the fried pork with garlic hot, garnished with some green onions if desired. It's a perfect dish for a weeknight dinner and it's also great as a tapa.

Pimientos de Padrón

Pimientos de Padrón, also known as Padrón peppers, are a popular dish in Spain, typically served as a tapa. These small green peppers are usually fried and served with a sprinkle of sea salt. They are typically mild in flavor, but occasionally a pepper can be quite spicy. Padrón peppers are a great way to showcase the flavors of Spain and they are also a great way to enjoy a simple and flavorful dish.

4 SERVINGS | **15 MINUTES** | **150 KCAL** | **EASY**

INGREDIENTS

- 1 pound of Padrón peppers
- 1/4 cup of olive oil
- Salt to taste

DIRECTIONS

1. Heat the olive oil in a large skillet over medium-high heat. The skillet should be large enough to accommodate the peppers without overcrowding. Once the oil is hot, it's time to add the peppers.
2. Carefully add the peppers to the skillet. Make sure not to overcrowd the skillet, as this will cause the peppers to steam instead of fry. If necessary, fry the peppers in batches.
3. Fry the peppers for about 2-3 minutes, or until they are blistered and slightly charred. This will give them a nice char and a smoky flavor, that will make them irresistible. Keep in mind that Padrón peppers are thin-skinned, so they will cook quickly.
4. Remove the peppers from the skillet and drain them on a paper towel-lined plate. This will help to remove any excess oil and it will also help to keep the peppers crispy.
5. Sprinkle the peppers with salt and serve hot. The salt will help to enhance the flavors of the peppers and it will also help to balance out the heat.
6. Serve these peppers as a tapa or an appetizer, they are perfect to share with friends and family. They are also a great addition to any Mediterranean-style meal.

Note: Keep in mind that Padrón peppers can be quite spicy, but they are usually mild. Be sure to try a pepper before eating a whole plate, so that you know what to expect.

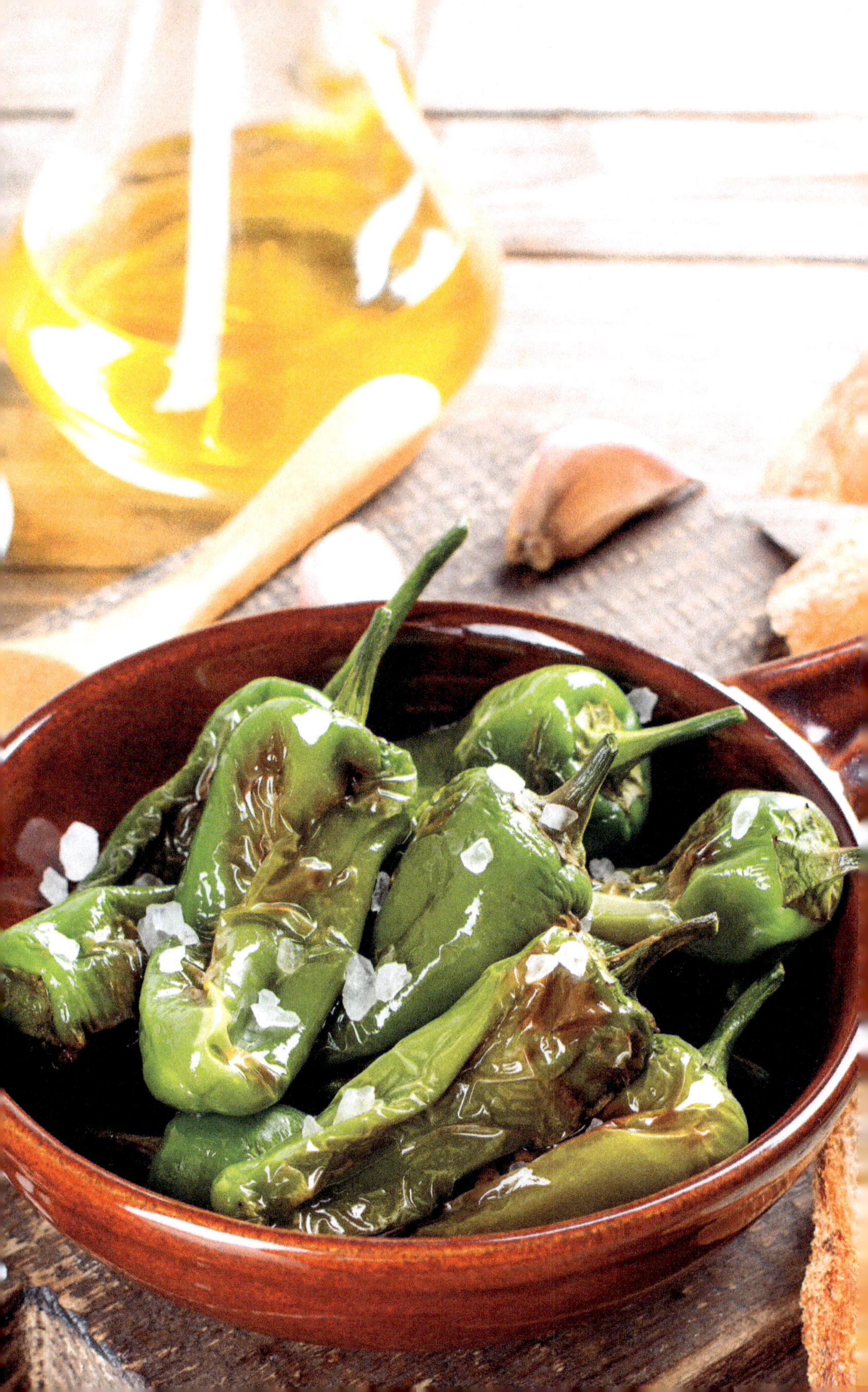

Ensalada de bacalao

Ensalada de Bacalao, also known as salt cod salad, is a classic Spanish dish that is typically made by combining salt cod, potatoes, and vegetables in a simple vinaigrette. It's a popular dish in Spain and it's often served as a tapa or a starter. The dish is a great way to showcase the flavors of Spain and it's also a great way to use up salt cod.

4 SERVINGS | **30 MINUTES** | **300 KCAL** | **EASY**

INGREDIENTS

- 1 pound of salt cod, soaked and flaked
- 2 potatoes, boiled and diced
- 1 red bell pepper, diced
- 1 onion, diced
- 2 cloves of garlic, minced
- 1/4 cup of olive oil
- 2 tablespoons of red wine vinegar
- Salt and pepper to taste
- Fresh parsley or thyme for garnish (optional)

DIRECTIONS

1. Soak the salt cod in cold water for 24 hours, changing the water every 8 hours, to remove the saltiness. Soaking the cod is an essential step to remove the saltiness and to make it more palatable. Soak it in a large enough bowl, to ensure that the cod is fully submerged.
2. Once the cod has been soaked, flake it into small pieces. It's important to flake it into small pieces, as this will make it easier to combine with the other ingredients.
3. In a large bowl, mix together the olive oil, red wine vinegar, minced garlic, salt, and pepper. This mixture will be your vinaigrette. The vinaigrette is simple but flavorful, it will help to bring all the ingredients together and it will also help to create a light and refreshing salad.
4. Add the flaked cod, diced potatoes, diced red bell pepper, and diced onion to the bowl and toss to coat well with the vinaigrette. Make sure that all the ingredients are well coated and that they have the chance to absorb all the flavors.
5. Let the salad sit in the refrigerator for at least 30 minutes, to allow the flavors to meld. This will help to enhance the flavors and it will also help to make the salad more refreshing.
6. Garnish with fresh parsley or thyme, if desired. This will add a fresh and herby note to the salad and it will also make it more appealing.

Note: Keep in mind that you can adjust the amount of red wine vinegar and olive oil to suit your taste. You can also add some sliced hard-boiled egg or tomato for a more flavorful dish.

Queso de cabra con miel

Queso de Cabra con Miel is a simple but delicious Spanish dish that combines creamy goat cheese with sweet honey. The dish is typically served as a starter or a tapa, and it's a great way to showcase the flavors of both the cheese and the honey. The dish is simple to make and it's a great way to enjoy a flavorful and satisfying meal.

4 SERVINGS — **10 MINUTES** — **200 KCAL** — **EASY**

INGREDIENTS

- 8 oz of goat cheese
- 1/4 cup of honey
- Fresh thyme or rosemary for garnish (optional)

DIRECTIONS

1. Cut the goat cheese into slices or wedges. Depending on your preference, you can cut the cheese into slices or wedges. This will make it easier to serve and it will also make it more visually appealing.
2. Heat the honey in a small saucepan over low heat. The honey should be heated just enough to make it pourable. This will make it easier to drizzle over the cheese and it will also help to infuse the cheese with the sweet and floral flavors of the honey.
3. Arrange the goat cheese slices or wedges on a serving plate. This will make it easier to serve and it will also make it more visually appealing.
4. Drizzle the warm honey over the cheese. The warm honey will help to infuse the cheese with the sweet and floral flavors of the honey and it will also help to create a delicious contrast of textures.
5. Garnish with fresh thyme or rosemary, if desired. The fresh herbs will add a fresh and herby note to the dish and it will also make it more visually appealing.
6. Serve immediately and enjoy the perfect combination of sweet and savory flavors. This dish is perfect to enjoy as a starter, a snack or a light lunch.

Note: Keep in mind that you can adjust the amount of honey to suit your taste. You can also serve the cheese with crackers or bread. And you can also try different variety of honey to get different flavor profile.

Cazuela de ajo

Cazuela de Ajo, also known as Garlic Soup, is a traditional Spanish soup that is typically made by combining garlic, bread, and broth. It's a popular dish in Spain and it's often served as a starter or a light meal. The dish is a great way to showcase the flavors of Spain and it's also a great way to enjoy a simple and flavorful soup.

4 SERVINGS | **30 MINUTES** | **150 KCAL** | **EASY**

INGREDIENTS

- 1 head of garlic, minced
- 4 cups of chicken or vegetable broth
- 4 slices of stale bread
- 1/4 cup of olive oil
- Salt and pepper to taste
- Fresh parsley or thyme for garnish (optional)

DIRECTIONS

1. In a large pot, heat the olive oil over medium heat. Add the minced garlic and sauté until fragrant. Be careful not to burn the garlic, as this will give the soup a bitter taste. The garlic is the star of this dish, so make sure to sauté it until it's fragrant and soft.
2. Add the broth to the pot and bring to a simmer. The broth will help to create a base for the soup and it will also help to infuse the soup with flavor.
3. Add the stale bread slices to the pot and stir to combine. The bread will help to thicken the soup and it will also give it a more substantial texture. As the bread sits in the soup, it will soften and break down, creating a thick, creamy soup.
4. Season the soup with salt and pepper to taste. The salt will help to enhance the flavors of the soup and the pepper will give it a nice kick.
5. Let the soup simmer for about 15 minutes, or until the bread is fully saturated and the soup has thickened. This will give the bread enough time to soften and break down and it will also allow the flavors to meld together.
6. Garnish with fresh parsley or thyme, if desired. The fresh herbs will add a fresh and herby note to the dish and it will also make it more visually appealing.
7. Serve hot and enjoy the comforting and flavorful soup. This dish is perfect to enjoy on a cold day or as a light lunch.

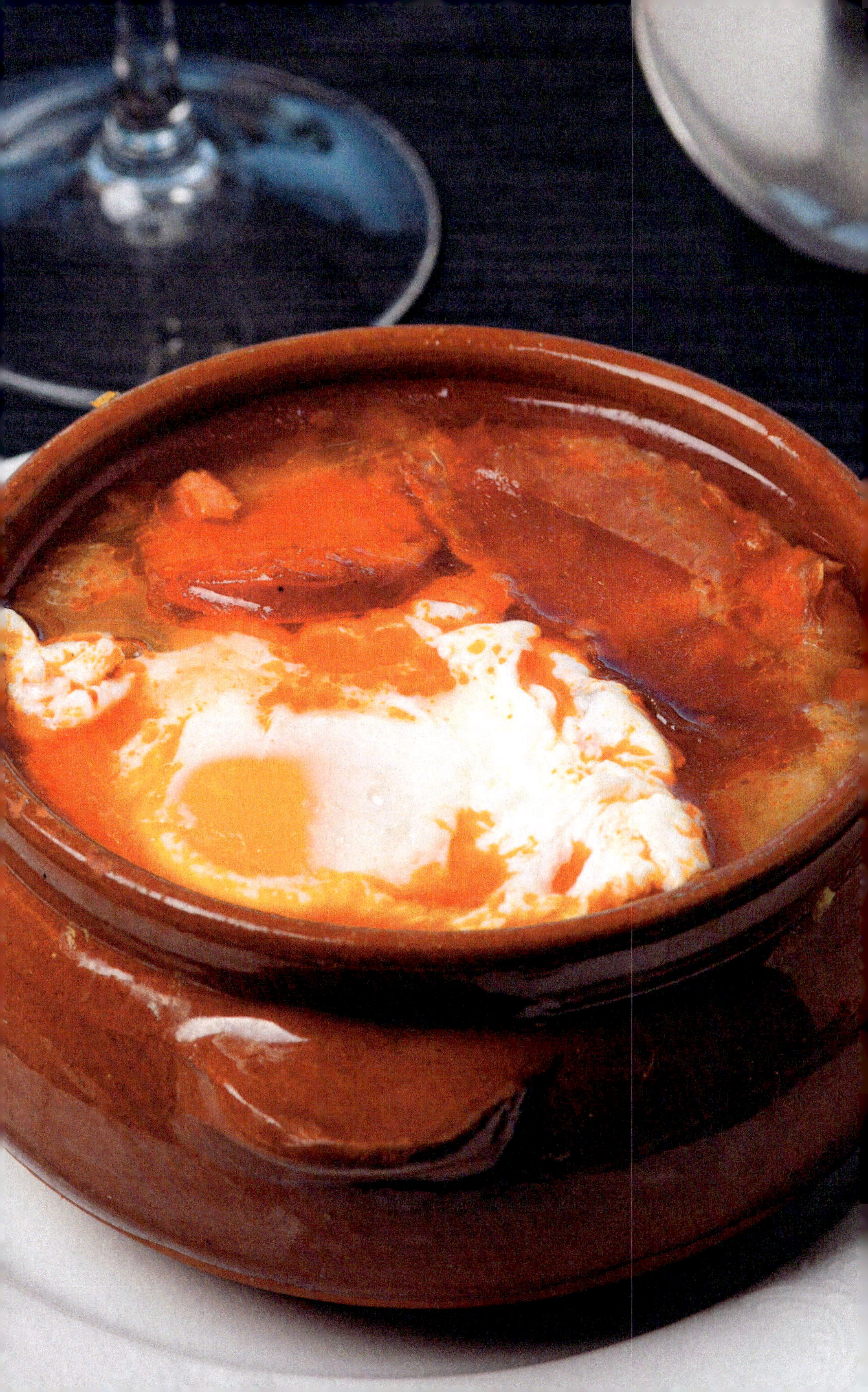

Huevos rotos

Huevos Rotos, also known as Broken Eggs, is a traditional Spanish dish that is typically made by frying an egg over a bed of potatoes. It's a popular dish in Spain and it's often served as a main course. The dish is a great way to showcase the flavors of Spain and it's also a great way to enjoy a simple and flavorful dish.

4 SERVINGS   **30 MINUTES**   **250 KCAL**   **EASY**

INGREDIENTS

- 1 lb of potatoes, peeled and sliced
- 4 cloves of garlic, minced
- 1/4 cup of olive oil
- Salt and pepper to taste
- 4 large eggs
- Fresh parsley or thyme for garnish (optional)

DIRECTIONS

1. In a large skillet, heat the olive oil over medium heat. Add the minced garlic and sauté until fragrant. Be careful not to burn the garlic, as this will give the dish a bitter taste. Garlic is a key ingredient in this dish and it should be sautéed until it's fragrant and soft in order to release its full flavor.
2. Add the sliced potatoes to the skillet and stir to combine. Make sure that the potatoes are evenly coated with the garlic and olive oil mixture.
3. Season the potatoes with salt and pepper to taste. The salt will help to enhance the flavors of the dish and the pepper will give it a nice kick.
4. Cook the potatoes for about 10-15 minutes, or until they are tender and golden brown. The potatoes will release moisture as they cook, so make sure to cook them until the moisture has evaporated and they are tender and golden brown.
5. Using a spoon, make a small well in the center of the potatoes. This will be the place for the eggs to be cracked.
6. Crack an egg into the well of each potato.
7. Cover the skillet and cook for 2-3 minutes or until the egg whites are set but the yolks are still runny. This will give you the perfect balance of runny yolk and crispy potatoes.
8. Garnish with fresh parsley or thyme, if desired. The fresh herbs will add a fresh and herby note to the dish and it will also make it more visually appealing.
9. Serve hot as a main course or a brunch dish. Enjoy the comforting and flavorful dish with the runny yolk and the crispy potatoes. This dish is perfect to enjoy as brunch or a light dinner.

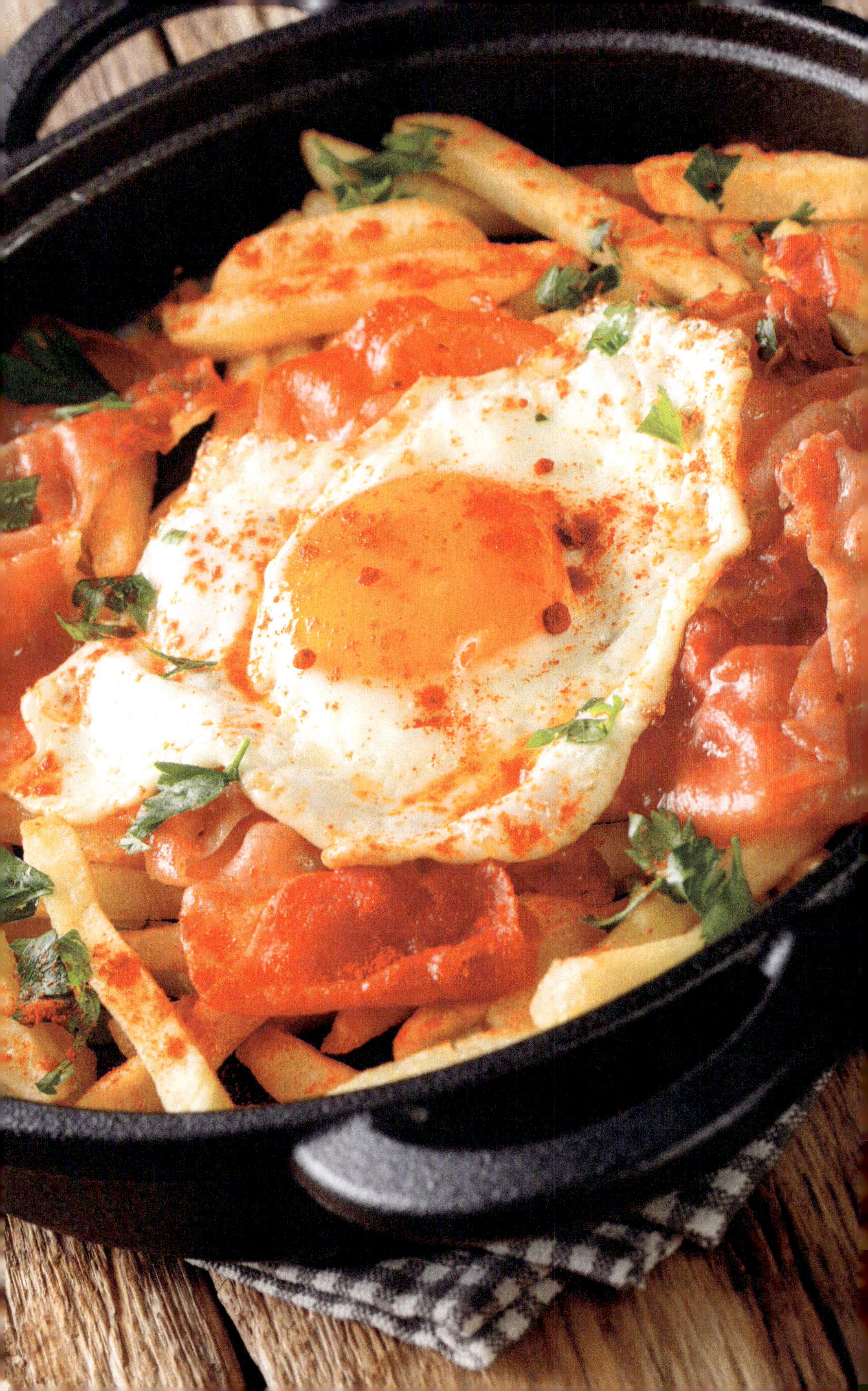

Champiñones al ajillo

Champiñones al Ajillo, also known as Garlic Mushroom, is a traditional Spanish dish that is typically made by sautéing mushrooms in a garlic and olive oil. It's a popular dish in Spain and it's often served as a side dish or a tapa. The dish is a great way to showcase the flavors of Spain and it's also a great way to enjoy a simple and flavorful dish.

4 SERVINGS | **15 MINUTES** | **150 KCAL** | **EASY**

INGREDIENTS

- 1 lb of mushrooms, sliced
- 4 cloves of garlic, minced
- 1/4 cup of olive oil
- Salt and pepper to taste
- Fresh parsley or thyme for garnish (optional)

DIRECTIONS

1. In a large skillet, heat the olive oil over medium heat. Add the minced garlic and sauté until fragrant. Be careful not to burn the garlic, as this will give the dish a bitter taste. Garlic is a key ingredient in this dish and it should be sautéed until it's fragrant and soft in order to release its full flavor.
2. Add the sliced mushrooms to the skillet and stir to combine. Make sure that the mushrooms are evenly coated with the garlic and olive oil mixture.
3. Season the mushrooms with salt and pepper to taste. The salt will help to enhance the flavors of the dish and the pepper will give it a nice kick.
4. Cook the mushrooms for about 5-8 minutes, or until they are tender and golden brown. The mushrooms will release moisture as they cook, so make sure to cook them until the moisture has evaporated and they are tender and golden brown.
5. Garnish with fresh parsley or thyme, if desired. The fresh herbs will add a fresh and herby note to the dish and it will also make it more visually appealing.
6. Serve hot as a side dish or a tapa. Enjoy the earthy and flavorful mushrooms with a nice and garlicky flavor. This dish is perfect to enjoy with your favorite meat dish or as a tapa with some bread.

Salmorejo

Salmorejo is a traditional Spanish cold soup originating from the southern region of Andalusia. It is similar to gazpacho but it's thicker and creamier due to the addition of bread. It is typically made with tomatoes, bread, garlic, olive oil, and vinegar. It's a popular dish in Spain and it's often served as a starter or a light meal. The dish is a great way to showcase the flavors of Spain and it's also a great way to enjoy a simple and flavorful dish.

4 SERVINGS **15 MINUTES** **250 KCAL** **EASY**

INGREDIENTS

- 1 lb of ripe tomatoes, peeled and seeded
- 1 slice of bread, crust removed
- 1 cloves of garlic, minced
- 1/4 cup of olive oil
- 2 tablespoons of sherry vinegar
- Salt and pepper to taste
- Fresh parsley or thyme for garnish (optional)

DIRECTIONS

1. In a blender, puree the tomatoes, bread, garlic, olive oil, and vinegar until smooth. Make sure that the tomatoes are peeled and seeded; this will make the soup creamy and smooth. The bread will also make the soup thicker and more satisfying.
2. Season the mixture with salt and pepper to taste. The salt will help to enhance the flavors of the dish and the pepper will give it a nice kick.
3. Transfer the mixture to a bowl and cover it with plastic wrap. Refrigerate overnight to allow the flavors to meld. This step is important as it allows the flavors to develop and it makes the soup more flavorful.
4. Before serving, adjust the seasoning if necessary. Taste the soup and adjust the seasoning accordingly.
5. Garnish with fresh parsley or thyme, if desired. The fresh herbs will add a fresh and herby note to the dish and it will also make it more visually appealing.
6. Serve cold as a starter or a light meal. Enjoy the refreshing and flavorful soup with a nice and garlicky flavor. Perfect to enjoy on a hot summer day or as a light meal.

Fabada asturiana

Fabada Asturiana is a traditional Spanish bean stew from the northern region of Asturias. It is typically made with large white beans, chorizo, morcilla, bacon, and pork shoulder. It's a hearty and comforting dish that is often served as a main course. Fabada Asturiana has a long history and it's considered as one of the most representative dishes of Asturian cuisine.

4 SERVINGS | **45 MINUTES** | **500 KCAL** | **MED**

INGREDIENTS

- 1 lb of large white beans, soaked overnight
- 1/2 lb of chorizo, cut into slices
- 1/2 lb of morcilla, cut into slices
- 1/4 lb of bacon, cut into cubes
- 1/4 lb of pork shoulder, cut into cubes
- 2 cloves of garlic, minced
- 1 onion, diced
- 1/4 cup of olive oil
- Salt and pepper to taste
- Fresh parsley or thyme for garnish (optional)

DIRECTIONS

1. In a large pot, heat the olive oil over medium heat. Add the minced garlic and onion and sauté until fragrant. The garlic and onion will add a nice depth of flavor and fragrance to the dish.
2. Add the pork shoulder, bacon, chorizo, and morcilla to the pot and cook for 5-7 minutes or until the meat is browned on all sides. The chorizo, morcilla and bacon will add a nice smoky and meaty flavor to the dish.
3. Drain the beans and add them to the pot. Add enough water to cover the beans and bring to a boil. The beans are the main ingredient of the dish and they will be the base of the stew.
4. Reduce the heat and let the stew simmer for 30-40 minutes or until the beans are tender and the stew is thickened. The stew should be thick and creamy, the beans should be tender and the meats should be cooked through.
5. Season the stew with salt and pepper to taste. Salt will enhance the flavors of the dish and pepper will give it a nice kick.
6. Garnish with fresh parsley or thyme, if desired. This step is optional but it will add a nice freshness and fragrance to the dish.
7. Serve hot as a main course. Enjoy the comforting and flavorful stew with the different meats and the tender beans. This dish is perfect for a cold winter day and it will warm you up and fill you up.

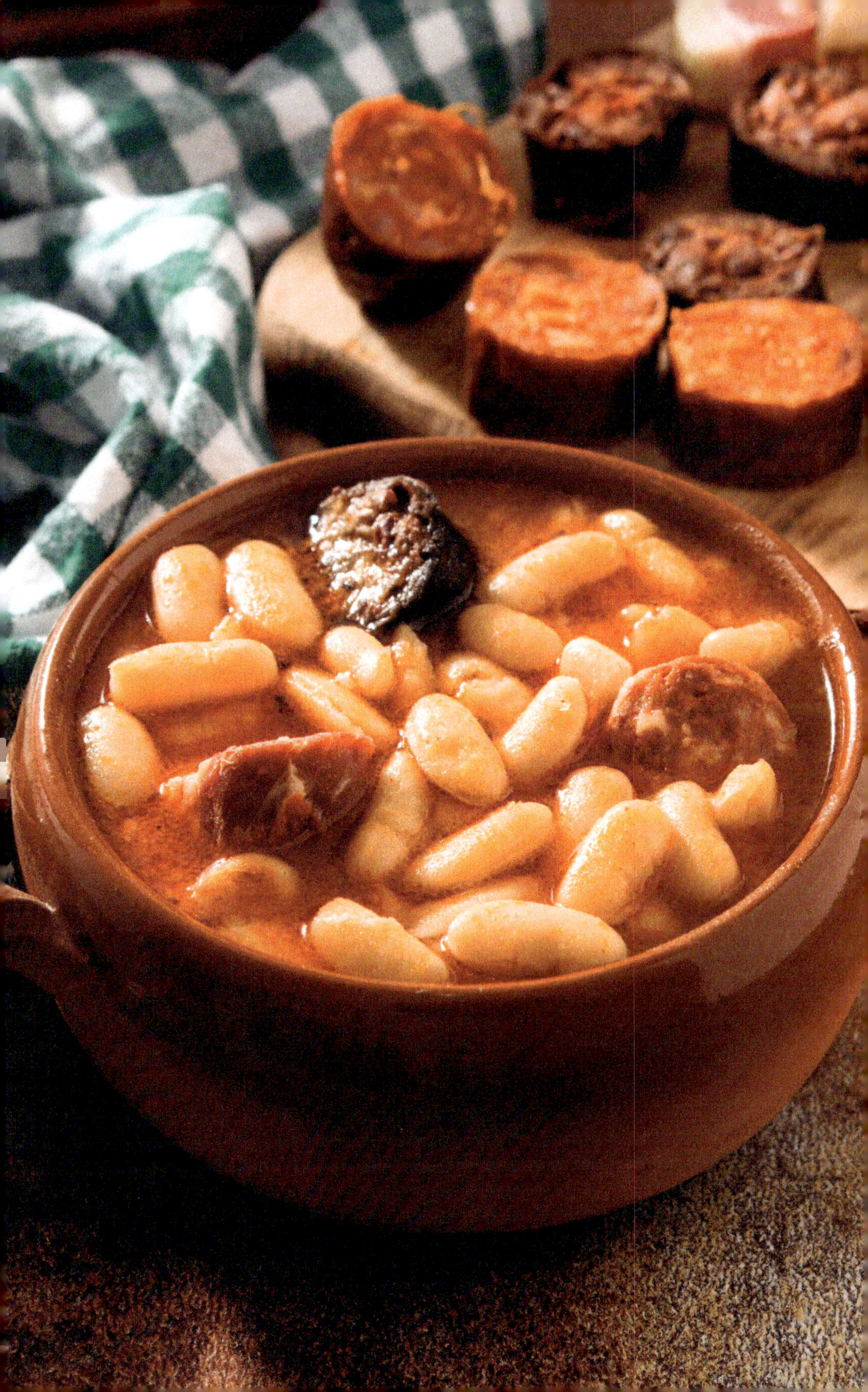

Sopa de lentejas

Sopa de lentejas is a traditional Spanish lentil soup that is hearty, comforting, and easy to make. This soup is perfect for a cold winter day, and it's packed with protein and fiber. It's a traditional dish from the region of Castilla-La Mancha.

4 SERVINGS **30 MINUTES** **250 KCAL** **EASY**

INGREDIENTS

- 1 cup of lentils
- 1 onion, diced
- 2 cloves of garlic, minced
- 2 carrots, diced
- 2 celery stalks, diced
- 2 potatoes, diced
- 4 cups of vegetable or chicken broth
- 1 tablespoon of olive oil
- Salt and pepper to taste
- Fresh parsley or cilantro for garnish

DIRECTIONS

1. Begin by rinsing the lentils thoroughly and picking out any small stones or debris. Set them aside.
2. In a large pot, heat the olive oil over medium heat. Add the diced onion and garlic and sauté until softened, about 5 minutes. The aroma of the garlic and onion will fill your kitchen and set the tone for a delicious dish.
3. Add the diced carrots, celery, and potatoes. Cook for another 5 minutes, stirring occasionally, until the vegetables have begun to soften and release their flavors.
4. Pour in the broth and bring the mixture to a boil. Reduce the heat to low, add the lentils and let it simmer for about 20 minutes or until the lentils are cooked through and the vegetables are tender.
5. Season with salt and pepper to taste, stirring occasionally.
6. Serve in bowls and garnish with fresh parsley or cilantro.
7. Enjoy your comforting and delicious sopa de lentejas! This hearty dish is perfect for a cold winter day, but it's also perfect for any time of the year. A great way to warm up and fill your stomach with a healthy, delicious and nutritious meal.

Pan con tomate

Pan con tomate, also known as tomato bread, is a traditional Spanish dish that is simple to make yet full of flavor. The dish consists of bread that is rubbed with fresh tomatoes, garlic, and olive oil. It is typically eaten as a breakfast or snack dish, and is also a popular tapa in Spanish bars and restaurants.

4 SERVINGS | **15 MINUTES** | **150 KCAL** | **EASY**

INGREDIENTS

- 4 slices of rustic bread
- 2 tomatoes, peeled and grated
- 2 cloves of garlic, minced
- 3 tablespoons of olive oil
- Salt and pepper to taste
- Fresh basil or parsley for garnish (optional)

DIRECTIONS

1. Preheat the oven to 350F.
2. Place the bread slices on a baking sheet and toast them in the oven for about 5-7 minutes or until they are golden brown and crispy. The toasting will give the bread a nice crunch and it will absorb the flavors better.
3. Remove the bread from the oven and let it cool for a few minutes.
4. In a small bowl, mix together the grated tomatoes, minced garlic, olive oil, salt and pepper.
5. Rub the tomato mixture over one side of the toasted bread slices, making sure to cover the surface evenly. The bread will absorb the tomato mixture and it will be infused with the flavors of the tomatoes, garlic, and olive oil.
6. Place the bread slices back on the baking sheet and return them to the oven. Bake for another 5-7 minutes or until the bread is crispy and the tomato mixture is heated through.
7. Garnish with fresh basil or parsley, if desired.
8. Serve warm as a breakfast or snack dish. Enjoy the simplicity and the delicious flavors of the bread infused with the tomatoes, garlic and olive oil. This dish is perfect for a quick and easy breakfast or a light snack and it will be a hit in any party.

CHAPTER 2

VALENCIA

Valencia is a region located on the eastern coast of Spain, known for its vibrant culture and delicious cuisine. The region is particularly famous for its paella, which is a traditional rice dish that originated in Valencia. Paella is typically made with a variety of meats or seafood, and is cooked over an open flame.

Another popular dish from Valencia is "Arroz al horno" (baked rice) which is a traditional dish that is cooked in the oven with a variety of meats and vegetables.

Valencia is also known for its fresh seafood, which is often used in dishes such as "suquet de peix" (fish stew) and "all i pebre" (garlic and pepper sauce).

The region also has a strong agricultural tradition, and as a result, many traditional Valencian dishes include fresh vegetables such as tomatoes, peppers, and eggplants. These ingredients can be found in dishes such as "gazpacho" and "encalada".

Valencia is also known for its "horchata" which is a sweet, refreshing beverage made from tiger nuts. This drink is typically served cold and is a popular refreshment during the hot summer months.

Valencia's cuisine is a perfect blend of traditional and modern flavors and ingredients, with a focus on fresh, seasonal ingredients and traditional cooking methods. Whether you're looking for a hearty paella or a refreshing horchata, the region has something to offer for everyone's taste. So if you have a chance to visit Valencia, don't miss the opportunity to try some of the delicious local dishes.

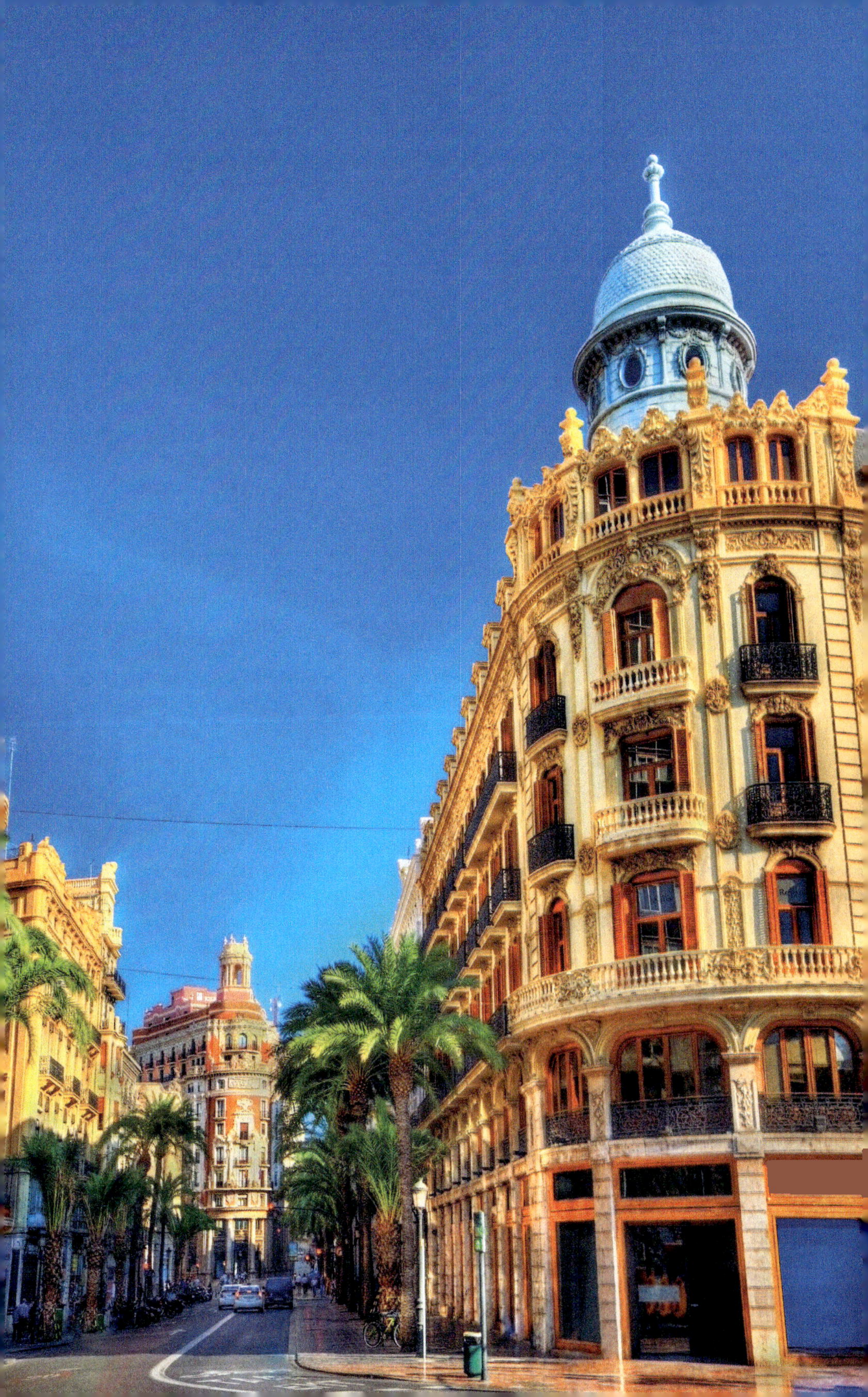

Did you know that...

1. Paella is a traditional dish from Valencia and is considered to be the most famous dish in Valencia cuisine. The original version of paella was made with rabbit, chicken, and snails, and cooked over an open fire. Today, there are many variations of paella, with seafood and vegetarian options available.
2. Horchata is a traditional drink in Valencia made from tiger nuts, water, and sugar. It is often served cold and is the perfect refreshment on a hot summer day. It is also a popular drink in some other parts of Spain and Latin America.
3. Valencia is known for its use of orange and lemon in its cuisine. Many traditional dishes use the zest and juice of these fruits to add a refreshing and unique flavor to the dish.
4. Valencia is one of the main producers of rice in Spain. The Albufera lake, located south of Valencia city, provides the perfect conditions for growing rice. The quality of the rice grown in the region is considered to be among the best in Spain.
5. The traditional sweet pastry from Valencia is known as "Fartons". These are small, sweet pastries that are often eaten with horchata. They are usually made with flour, sugar, and yeast, and shaped like a long, thin strip.
6. Valencia is also known for its many festivals, including the famous Las Fallas festival, where giant sculptures made of paper mache are displayed throughout the city and then burned. The festival also includes traditional foods like "Paella Valenciana".
7. Valencia is a coastal city and therefore seafood plays a big role in the cuisine. Some of the most popular seafood dishes include "Arroz a banda" (rice with fish) and "All i pebre" (octopus with a sauce made of garlic, olive oil, and paprika).
8. Valencia is also known for its almond groves and therefore, many traditional dishes use almonds in various forms such as "Agua de Valencia" which is a cocktail made of orange juice, champagne and cava, and vodka.
9. Valencia cuisine has influences from the Mediterranean, which is why it is known for its use of herbs and spices such as saffron, rosemary, and thyme.
10. Valencia cuisine is also known for its sweet pastries, many of which are made with puff pastry and filled with cream or chocolate. Some of the most popular pastries include "Cocas" and "Canyelles".

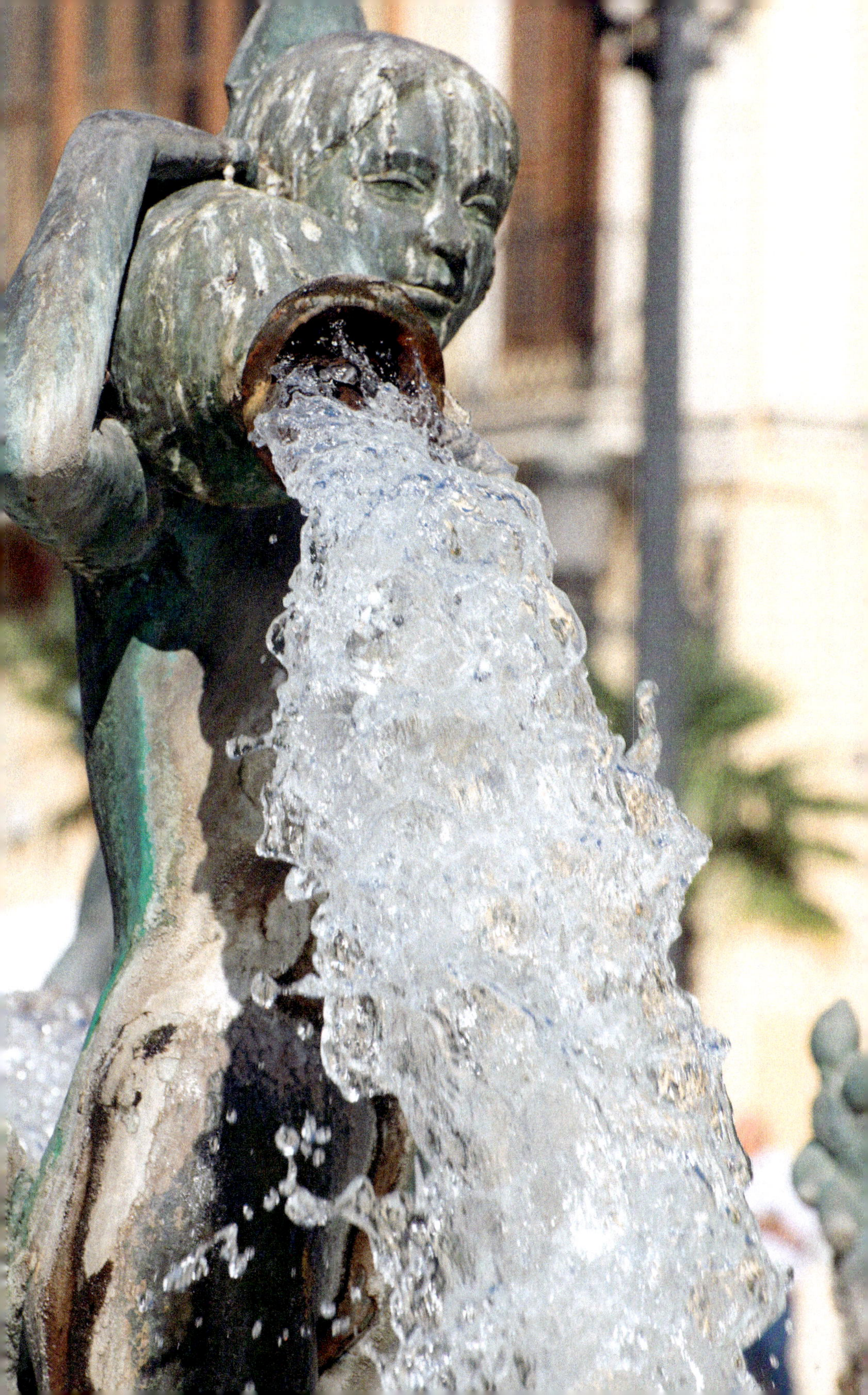

Paella valenciana

Paella Valenciana is a traditional Spanish dish from the region of Valencia. It is a rice dish that typically includes chicken, rabbit, green beans, and sometimes snails. The dish is traditionally cooked in a paella pan over an open fire. It is a popular dish served at family gatherings, festivals, and special occasions. The dish is considered a cultural icon of Valencia.

4 SERVINGS | **45 MINUTES** | **600 KCAL** | **MED**

INGREDIENTS

- 1 lb of chicken, cut into pieces
- 1 lb of rabbit, cut into pieces
- 1 onion, diced
- 2 cloves of garlic, minced
- 1 red pepper, diced
- 1 cup of green beans, trimmed
- 1/2 cup of diced tomatoes
- 2 cups of chicken stock
- 1 cup of short-grain rice
- 1/4 cup of chopped parsley
- 1 tsp of saffron threads
- Salt and pepper to taste
- Olive oil

DIRECTIONS

1. Heat olive oil in a paella pan or a large skillet over medium heat. Add the chicken and rabbit, and sauté until browned. Remove the meat from the pan and set aside.
2. In the same pan, add the onion, garlic, and red pepper, and sauté until softened.
3. Add the green beans, diced tomatoes, and saffron, and stir to combine.
4. Add the chicken stock and bring the mixture to a boil.
5. Add the rice and stir to combine.
6. Reduce the heat to low and return the meat to the pan. Cover and simmer for 18-20 minutes, or until the rice is cooked through and the liquid has been absorbed.
7. Remove the pan from the heat and let it sit for a few minutes before serving.
8. Sprinkle chopped parsley on top before serving.

Paella Valenciana is a delicious and comforting meal that is perfect for sharing with family and friends. It is a traditional dish that is steeped in history and culture, and it is sure to impress your guests.

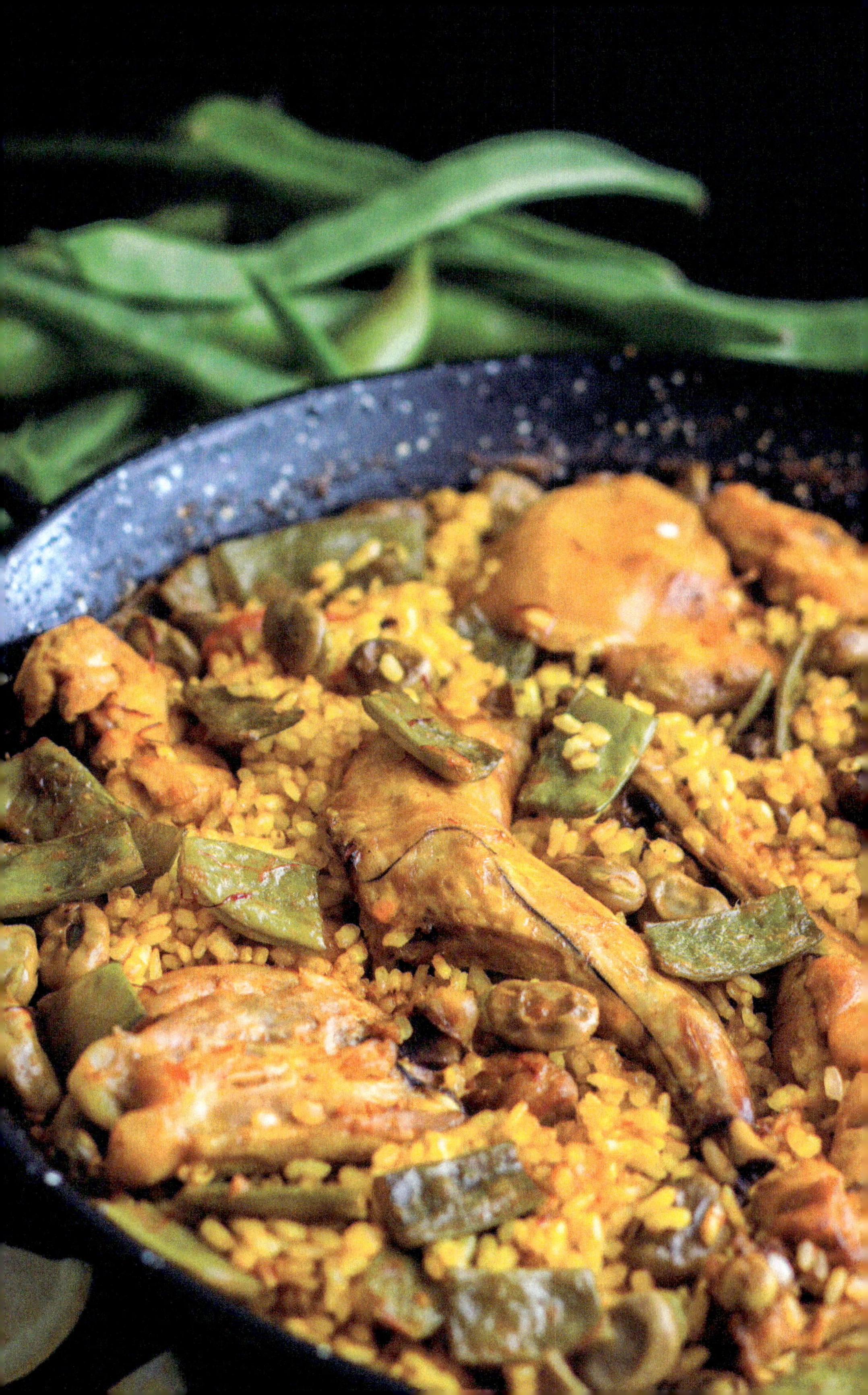

All i pebre

This is a traditional dish from the Valencia region of Spain. The name of the dish literally translates to "garlic and pepper" in Catalan. It is a simple and flavorful dish that consists of eels cooked in a sauce made of garlic, olive oil, and chili pepper.

4 SERVINGS | **30 MINUTES** | **300 KCAL** | **EASY**

INGREDIENTS

- 1 lb of eel
- 1 head of garlic, finely chopped
- 1 tsp of chili pepper flakes
- 1/2 cup of olive oil
- Salt and pepper to taste

DIRECTIONS

1. First, prepare the garlic and chili pepper. Peel and chop the garlic cloves and finely chop the chili pepper.
2. In a large skillet, heat the olive oil over medium heat. Once the oil is hot, add the garlic and chili pepper and cook for 1-2 minutes, until fragrant.
3. Next, add the eel to the skillet and cook for 5-7 minutes, until the eel is cooked through. Remove the eel from the skillet and set it aside.
4. In the same skillet, add the diced tomatoes and cook for 5-7 minutes, until they are softened and have released their juices.
5. While the tomatoes are cooking, cut the eel into bite-sized pieces.
6. Once the tomatoes are cooked, add the eel back to the skillet along with the salt and pepper. Stir everything together and cook for an additional 2-3 minutes to let the flavors meld together.
7. To finish the dish, add the chopped parsley to the skillet and give everything a final stir.
8. Serve the all i pebre in bowls and enjoy with a slice of toasted bread.

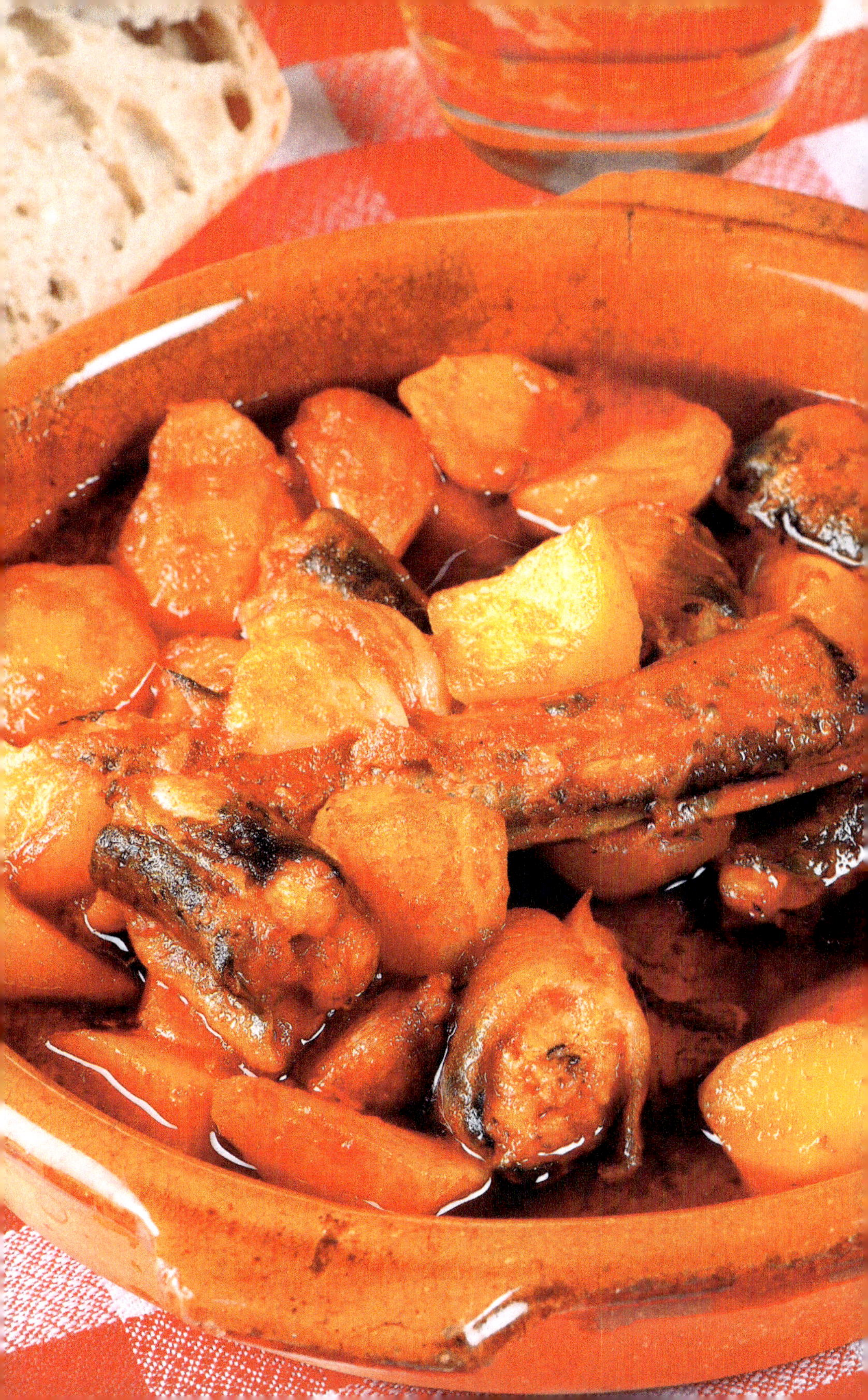

Esgarraet

Esgarraet is a traditional dish from Valencia, Spain, typically made with a combination of red bell peppers and cod fish. The dish is believed to have originated in the coastal towns of Valencia, where it was typically served as a tapa or a light meal.

4 SERVINGS | **20 MINUTES** | **250 KCAL** | **EASY**

INGREDIENTS

- 4 red bell peppers
- 2 medium-sized cod fish fillets
- 2 cloves of garlic
- 2 tablespoons of olive oil
- Salt and pepper to taste

DIRECTIONS

1. Start by cleaning and slicing the red bell peppers and the onions.
2. Heat up a large skillet over medium-high heat. Once hot, add the olive oil and the sliced vegetables. Sauté for a few minutes until they start to soften.
3. Add the sliced cod fish to the skillet and mix it well with the vegetables. Add in the diced tomatoes and the paprika. Stir everything together until the cod fish starts to flake apart.
4. Reduce the heat to medium-low and let the mixture simmer for about 10 minutes, or until the vegetables are fully cooked and the sauce has thickened. Stir occasionally to prevent sticking.
5. Remove from heat and let it cool for a few minutes. Finally, add a drizzle of olive oil, a sprinkle of salt, and a sprinkle of parsley.
6. Serve it warm with a slice of bread or with a side dish of your choice, and enjoy the unique blend of flavors that Esgarraet di Valencia has to offer!

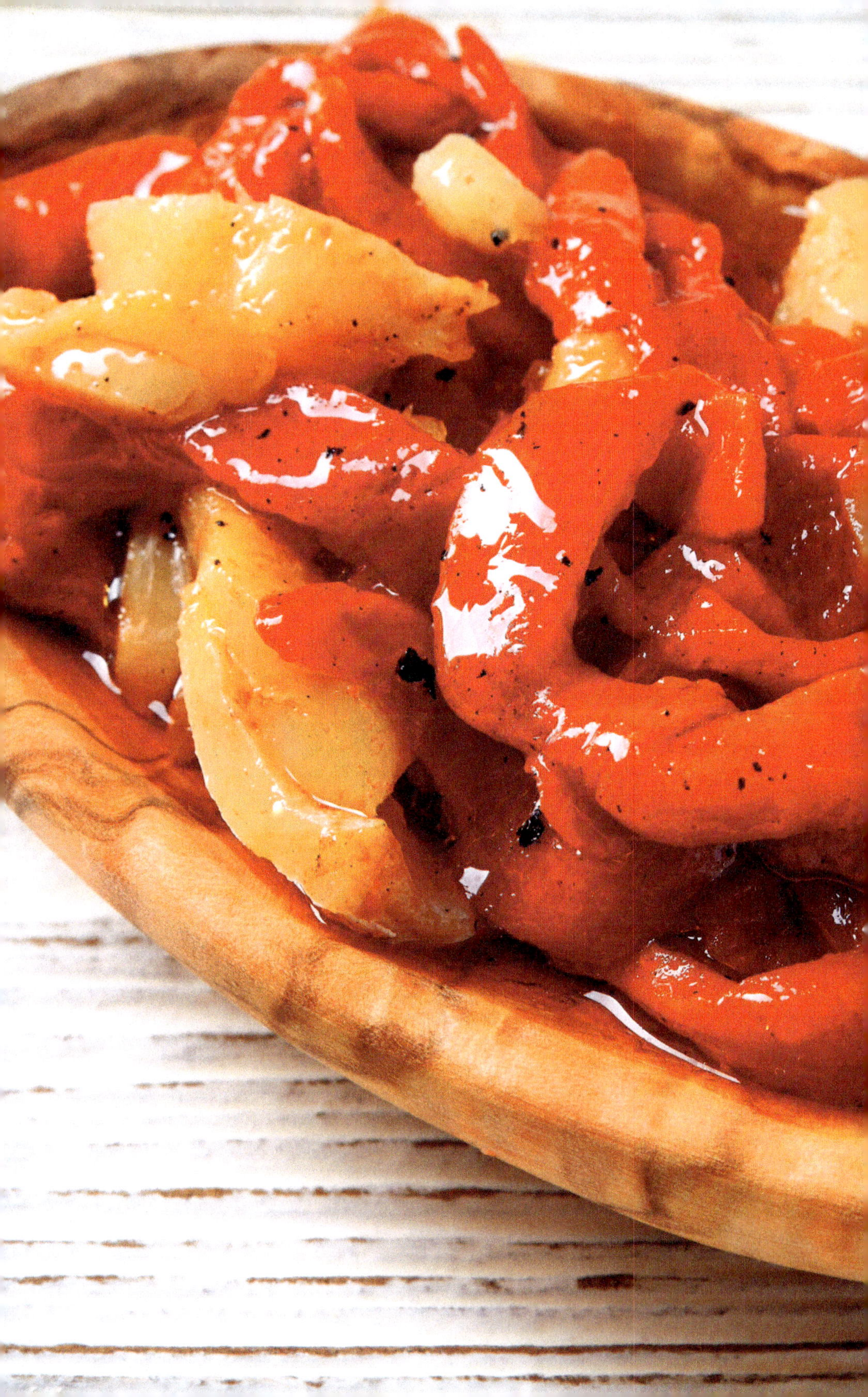

Fideuà

Fideuà di Valencia, also known as Fideuà a la valenciana, is a traditional Valencian dish that originated in the region of Valencia, Spain. It is a variation of the famous paella, but it is made with short, thin noodles called "fideus" instead of rice. The dish is typically cooked with seafood and vegetables, and is usually served as a main course. The dish has been a staple in the Valencian cuisine for centuries and is typically served in a large, shallow pan called a "paellera" which is unique to the Valencian region.

4 SERVINGS | **45 MINUTES** | **350 KCAL** | **MED**

INGREDIENTS

- 1 pound of short, thin noodles (fideus)
- 1 pound of mixed seafood (such as squid, shrimp, and mussels)
- 1 onion, finely chopped
- 2 cloves of garlic, minced
- 1 red bell pepper, diced
- 1 cup of green beans, trimmed
- 4 cups of fish stock or water
- 1/2 cup of olive oil
- Salt and pepper to taste
- 1/4 cup of chopped parsley for garnish

DIRECTIONS

1. In a large paellera or skillet, heat the olive oil over medium heat.
2. Add the onion, garlic, and red bell pepper and sauté until the vegetables are soft and translucent.
3. Add the green beans and sauté for another minute.
4. Add the mixed seafood and sauté for 2-3 minutes, or until the seafood is partially cooked.
5. Add the fish stock or water to the pan and bring it to a simmer.
6. Add the noodles and stir well, making sure that the noodles are evenly distributed and covered by the liquid.
7. Season with salt and pepper to taste.
8. Bring the mixture to a boil, then reduce the heat to low, cover the pan and let it simmer for 15-20 minutes, or until the noodles are cooked through and the liquid has been absorbed.
9. Remove the pan from heat and let it sit for a few minutes before serving.
10. Garnish with chopped parsley and serve hot.

Note: Some variations of Fideuà di Valencia recipe may also include chicken or rabbit meat, which is cooked with the vegetables and seafood. This is a traditional version of the dish, you can add or remove ingredients as per your preference.

Arròs negre

Arròs Negre is a traditional Spanish dish from Catalonia, typically made with short-grain rice, squid ink, and seafood. The dish gets its characteristic black color from the squid ink, which also adds a unique, subtle briny flavor. It's a popular dish in coastal regions, and it's often served as a main course.

4 SERVINGS **30 MINUTES** **450 KCAL** **HARD**

INGREDIENTS

- 1 lb of seafood (squid, shrimp, and mussels)
- 1 onion, diced
- 2 cloves of garlic, minced
- 1 cup of short-grain rice
- 2 cups of fish stock
- 1/2 cup of white wine
- 2 tbsp of squid ink
- 1/4 cup of chopped parsley
- Salt and pepper to taste
- Olive oil

DIRECTIONS

1. Heat olive oil in a paella pan or a large skillet over medium heat. Add the onion and garlic, and sauté until softened.
2. Add the seafood and cook until it turns pink, about 5 minutes. Remove the seafood from the pan and set aside.
3. Add the rice to the pan and stir to coat the grains with oil. Cook for 2-3 minutes until the rice becomes translucent.
4. Add the white wine and stir, allowing the alcohol to evaporate.
5. Add the fish stock, squid ink, salt, and pepper, and bring the mixture to a boil.
6. Reduce the heat to low and cover the pan. Simmer for 18-20 minutes, or until the rice is cooked through.
7. Return the seafood to the pan, and stir in the chopped parsley.
8. Let the rice sit for a few minutes before serving to allow the flavors to meld together.
9. Serve it hot and enjoy the delicious black rice with a touch of seafood flavor. It's a perfect meal for a special occasion or when you want to impress your guests.

CHAPTER 3

MADRID

Madrid is the capital of Spain and it is known for its rich culinary heritage and diverse food culture. The city is home to a wide variety of traditional dishes and modern fusion cuisine.

One of the most popular dishes in Madrid is "Cocido Madrileño", a traditional stew made with chickpeas, vegetables, and meats such as pork and beef. It is typically served with a side of "galletas" (crackers) and is a must-try for those who want to experience the authentic flavors of Madrid.

Another popular dish is "Callos a la Madrileña" which is a traditional pork dish made with pork tripe, chorizo, and morcilla (blood sausage). It's a hearty and flavorful dish that is typically served as a main course.

Madrid is also known for its "Huevos rotos" (broken eggs) which is a dish made of fried eggs served over a bed of fried potatoes, with a side of jamón ibérico (Iberian ham) or chorizo.

The city is also famous for its tapas bars, where you can find a wide variety of traditional and modern dishes such as "patatas bravas" (spicy fried potatoes) and "croquetas" (deep-fried balls of béchamel sauce and various fillings).

Madrid is also home to a vibrant street food scene, where you can find traditional dishes such as "churros" (deep-fried dough) and "torrijas" (Spanish-style French toast).

Madrid's cuisine perfectly blends traditional and modern flavors and ingredients, focusing on fresh, seasonal ingredients and traditional cooking methods. Whether you're looking for a hearty stew or a refreshing tapas, the city has something to offer for everyone's taste. So if you have a chance to visit Madrid, don't miss the opportunity to try some of the delicious local dishes.

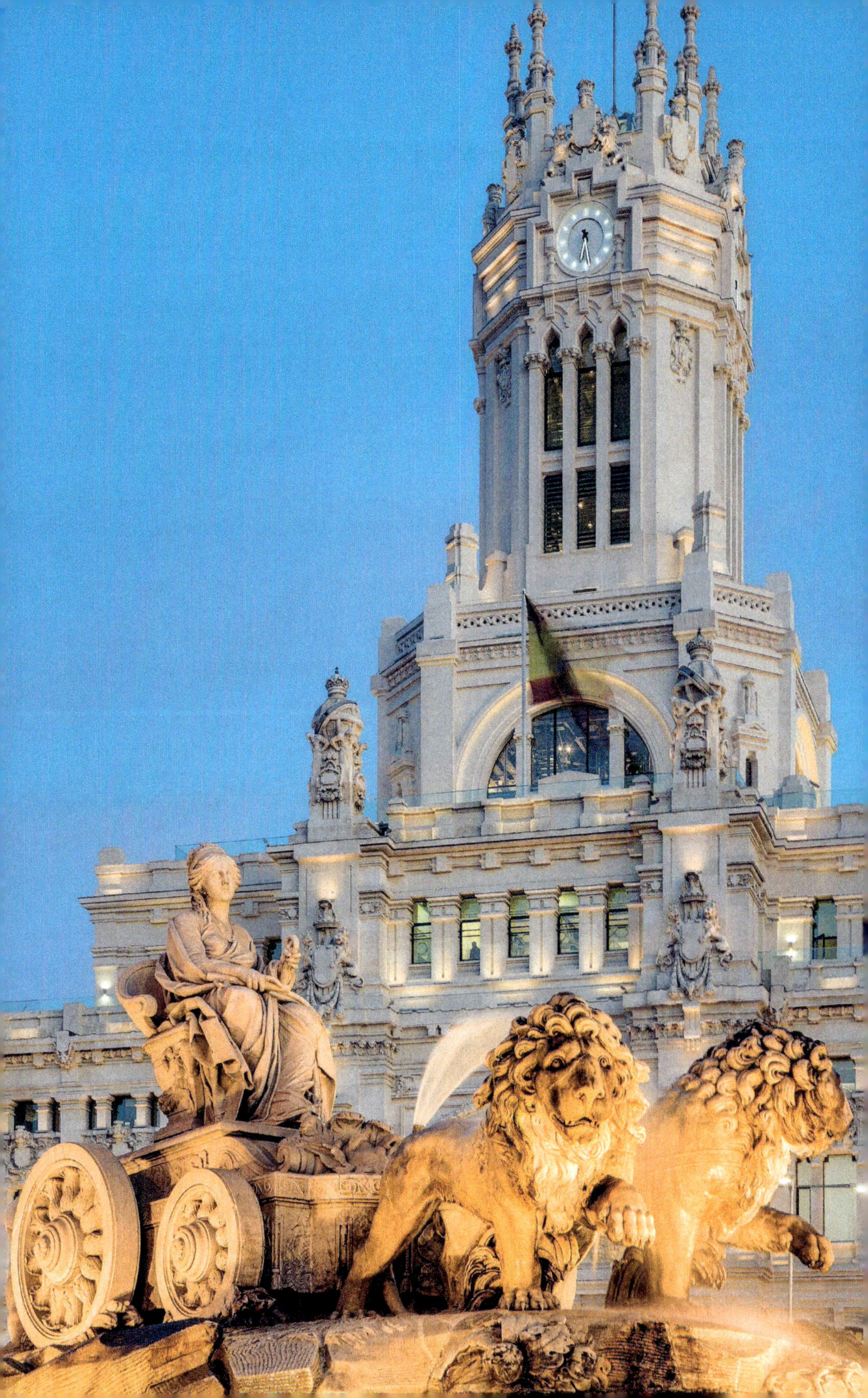

Did you know that...

1. Cocido Madrileño is a traditional stew that is considered to be the most famous dish in Madrid cuisine. It is made with chickpeas, vegetables, and meats like pork, beef, chicken, and chorizo. It is often served with a side of noodles or bread.
2. Callos a la Madrileña is another traditional stew dish, made with pork tripe, chorizo, and morcilla (blood sausage). It is a hearty dish that is often served in winter.
3. Huevos rotos, or "broken eggs," is a popular dish in Madrid. It consists of fried eggs served over a bed of fried potatoes and is often topped with a meat such as jamón or chorizo.
4. Madrid is known for its tapas, or small plates of food. Some popular tapas in Madrid include tortilla española, croquetas, and patatas bravas.
5. Madrid is also known for its fresh seafood, particularly its anchovies and sardines. These small fish are often served marinated, grilled, or in a traditional dish such as boquerones en vinagre.
6. Madrid is home to many traditional taverns, called "tabernas", where you can find typical dishes like "Sopa Castellana" (a traditional soup from Castilla) and "Callos" (a stew made with pork tripe, chorizo and morcilla)
7. Madrid has a long tradition of preserving food, which is why it is famous for its charcuterie. Spanish cured meats such as jamón ibérico and chorizo are known for their rich, intense flavor and are often served as tapas.
8. Madrid's cuisine is known for its hearty and rich dishes, which are perfect for the colder winter months. Some popular winter dishes include Cocido Madrileño and Callos a la Madrileña.
9. The city is also known for its wide variety of desserts and sweet pastries. Some popular pastries include "Churros" which are a fried dough pastry often served with a chocolate dipping sauce, and "Tocinillo de cielo" a traditional dessert made with egg yolks, sugar, and flour.
10. Madrid is home to many restaurants and bars, including some of the most famous Michelin-starred restaurants in Spain. The city's culinary scene is constantly evolving and offers a diverse range of options, from traditional taverns to modern and experimental restaurants.

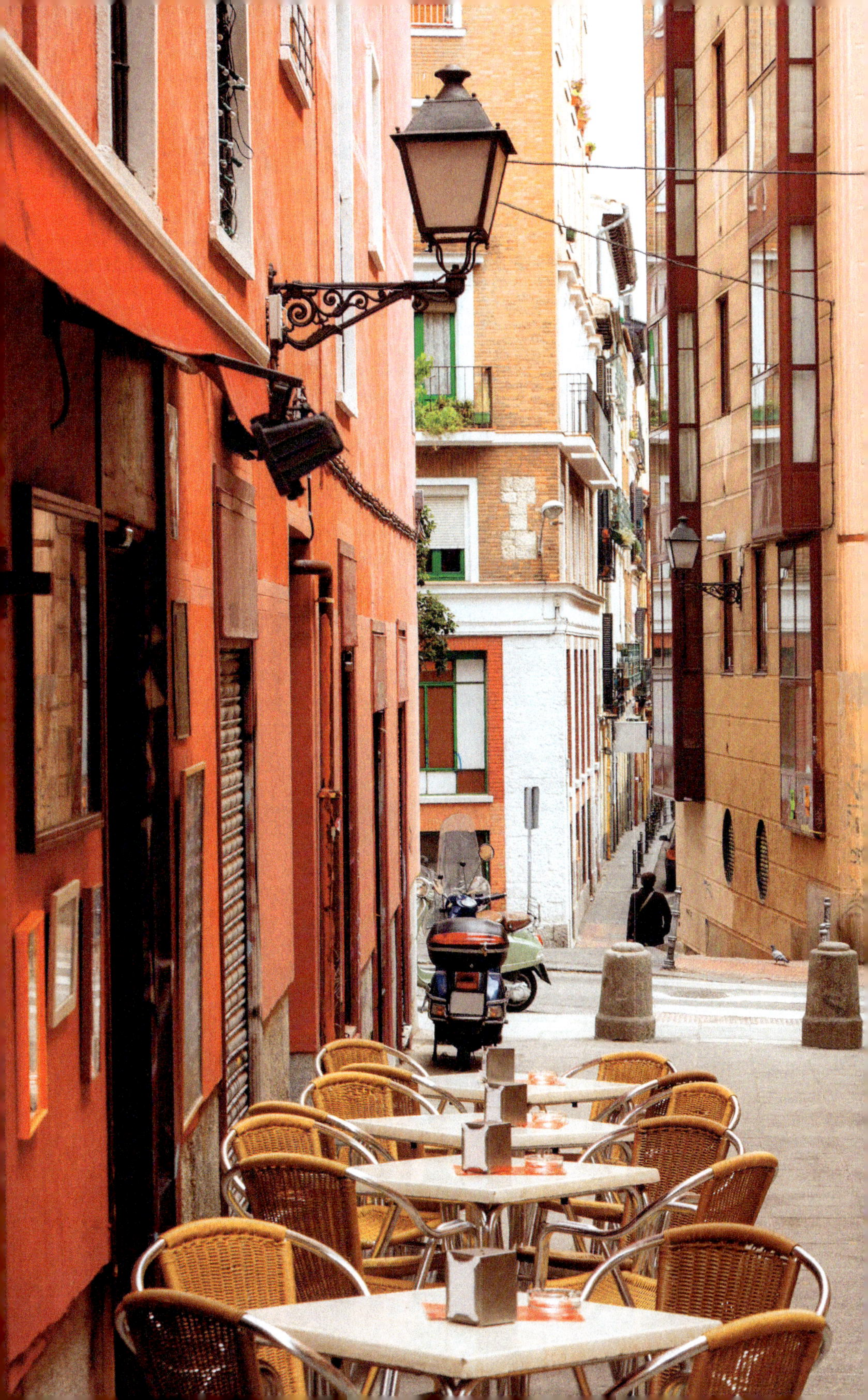

Huevos rotos con jamón

"Huevos rotos" is a classic Spanish dish that consists of broken fried eggs served over a bed of fried potatoes. This variation, "huevos rotos con jamón di Madrid," adds a touch of Madrid flavor by topping the dish with thin slices of jamón serrano, a type of cured ham that is a staple in the region. This dish is perfect for a hearty breakfast or brunch.

4 SERVINGS | **20 MINUTES** | **700 KCAL** | **EASY**

INGREDIENTS

- 4 medium potatoes
- 8 large eggs
- Salt and pepper
- 8 thin slices of jamón serrano
- Olive oil

DIRECTIONS

1. Begin by heating a large skillet over medium-high heat. Add enough oil to coat the bottom of the pan, and let it heat up for a minute or two.
2. While the oil is heating, thinly slice the jamón serrano and set it aside.
3. Crack the eggs into a bowl and beat them lightly with a fork. Season with a pinch of salt and pepper.
4. Once the oil is hot, add the sliced jamón serrano to the pan and cook for 1-2 minutes, until it starts to crisp up.
5. Using a slotted spoon, remove the jamón from the pan and set it aside.
6. Add the beaten eggs to the pan, and use a spatula to gently stir and scramble the eggs.
7. Once the eggs are cooked through, but still slightly runny, remove the pan from the heat and add the cooked jamón serrano back to the pan.
8. Serve immediately, with some crusty bread on the side. The eggs and jamón should be served on top of the bread.
9. Enjoy your Huevos rotos con jamón di Madrid, a classic and delicious Madridian dish that is perfect for any time of day!

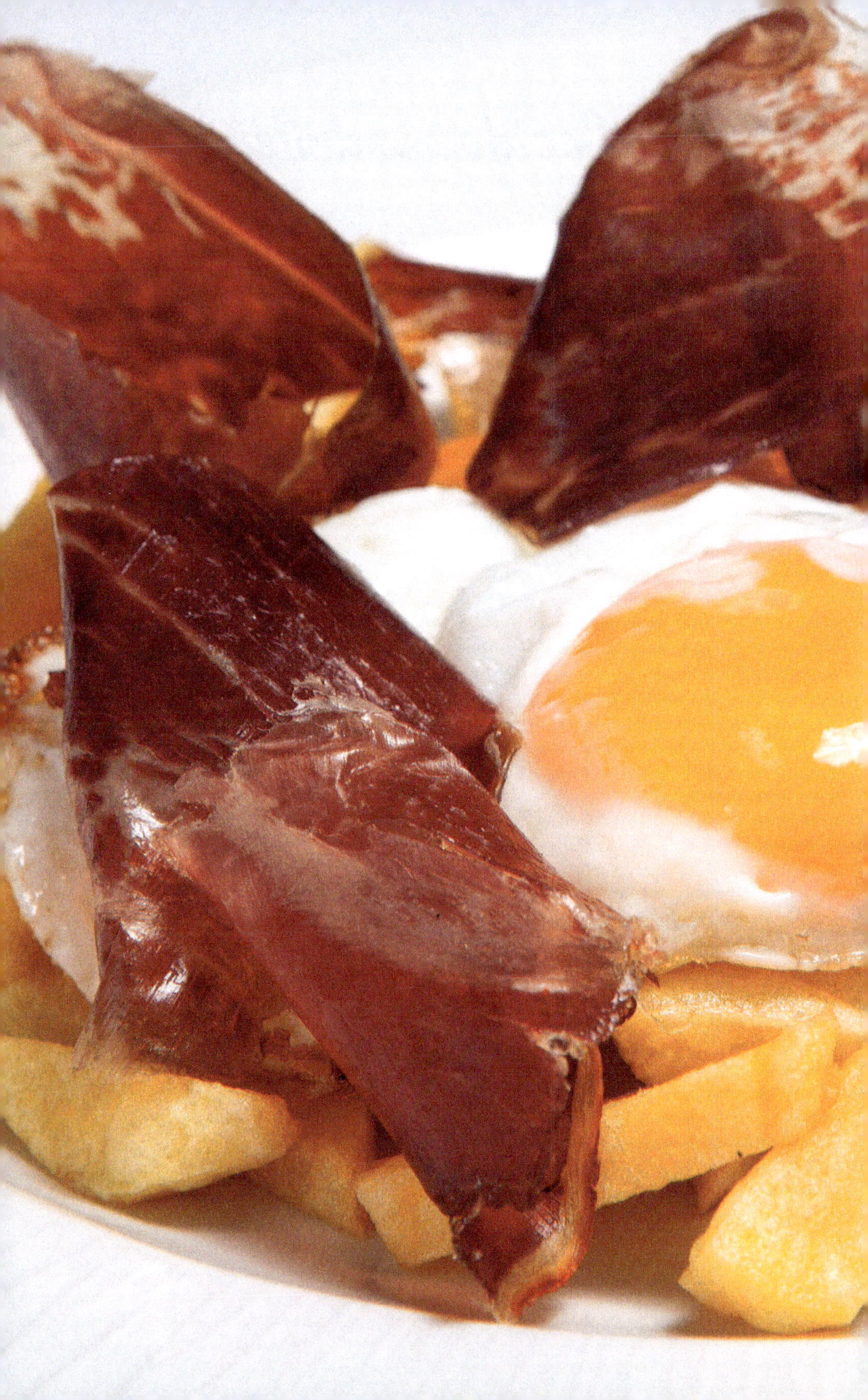

Cocido madrileño

Cocido Madrileño is a traditional stew hailing from the Madrid region of Spain. It is a hearty and comforting dish that is typically served in the winter months. The dish is made with a variety of meats, chickpeas, and vegetables, and is often served with a side of crusty bread to soak up the rich, flavorful broth. Cocido Madrileño is considered a staple of Madrid cuisine, and has a long history dating back to the Middle Ages.

4 SERVINGS   **18 MINUTES**   **450 KCAL**   **HARD**

INGREDIENTS

- 1 lb chickpeas, soaked overnight
- 1 lb beef shank
- 1 lb pork shoulder
- 1 lb chorizo
- 1 lb morcilla (blood sausage)
- 1 onion, diced
- 2 cloves garlic, minced
- 1 head of cabbage, cut into wedges
- 2 carrots, peeled and diced
- 2 potatoes, peeled and diced
- 2 cups of chicken broth
- salt and pepper to taste
- olive oil

DIRECTIONS

1. Start by soaking the chickpeas overnight in a large pot of water. Drain and rinse them the next day.
2. In a large pot or casserole, bring the chickpeas to a boil with enough water to cover them by about 2 inches.
3. Add the pork belly, chorizo, and morcilla to the pot.
4. Once the water comes to a boil, reduce the heat and let the stew simmer for about 1 hour or until the chickpeas are tender.
5. Add the cabbage and the potatoes to the pot and continue to simmer for an additional 30-40 minutes or until the vegetables are tender.
6. Season the stew with salt and pepper to taste and serve hot with some crusty bread.
7. It's traditional to serve Cocido Madrileño in 3 courses. First, the broth and vegetables, then the meats and chickpeas, and finally the chickpeas and vegetables together.
8. Enjoy your hearty and comforting Cocido Madrileño!

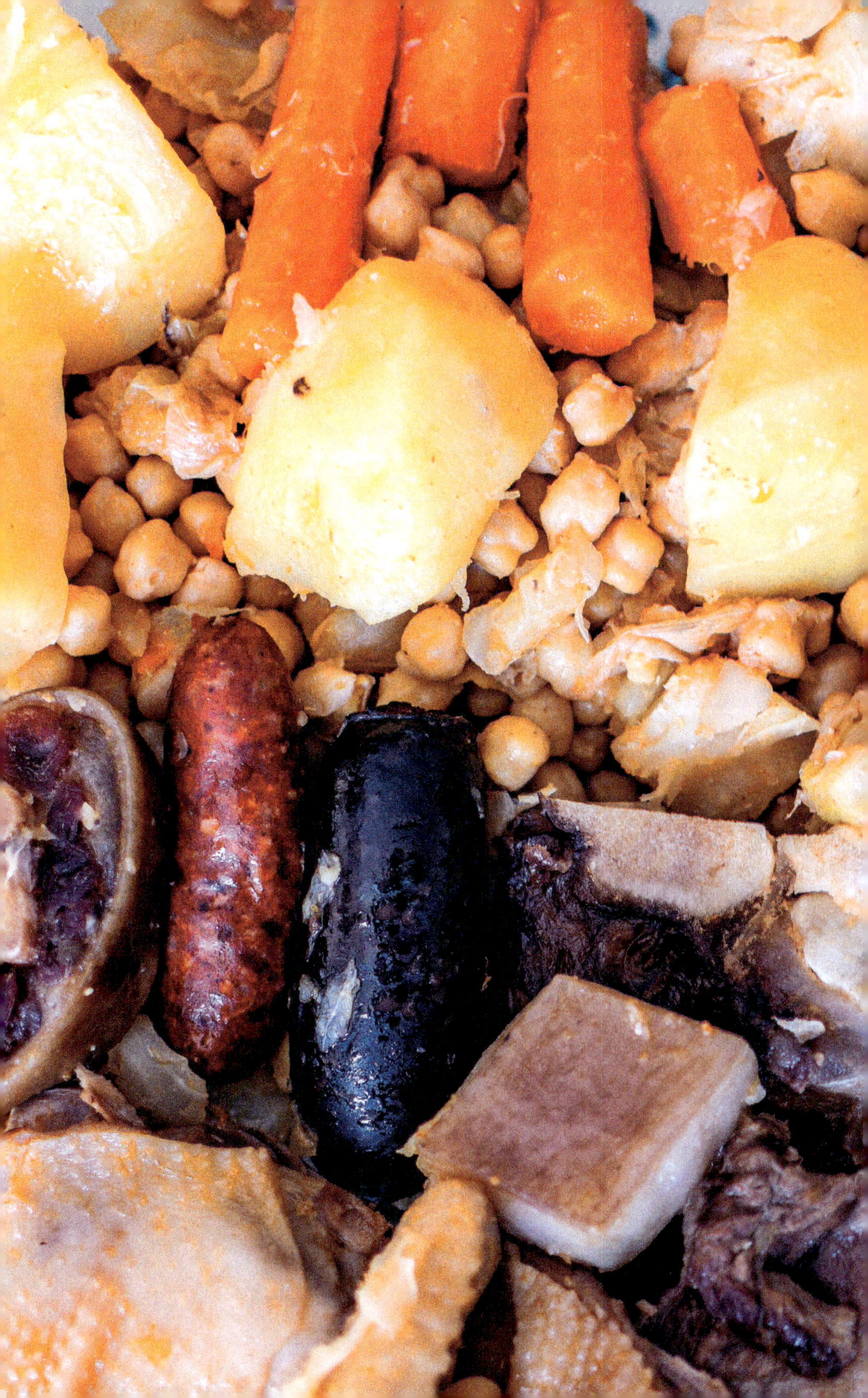

Callos a la madrileña

Callos a la madrileña is a traditional dish from Madrid, Spain. It is a hearty stew made with pork stomach, chickpeas, chorizo, and morcilla (blood sausage). This dish has a rich history, dating back to the 19th century, and is considered a classic of Madrid's cuisine.

4 SERVINGS | **90 MINUTES** | **500 KCAL** | **MED**

INGREDIENTS

- 2 lbs pork stomach, cleaned and cut into small cubes
- 1 lb chickpeas, soaked overnight
- 1 lb chorizo, sliced
- 1 lb morcilla (blood sausage), sliced
- 2 onions, diced
- 4 cloves of garlic, minced
- 2 cups chicken broth
- 2 cups water
- 2 tbsp olive oil
- Salt and pepper to taste
- 1 tbsp pimenton (smoked paprika)

DIRECTIONS

1. In a large pot or casserole, heat the olive oil over medium heat. Add the diced onions and garlic, and cook until translucent.
2. Add the pork stomach to the pot and stir well. Cook for 5 minutes, or until the pork stomach starts to brown.
3. Add the sliced chorizo and morcilla to the pot, and stir well. Cook for another 5 minutes.
4. Add the soaked chickpeas to the pot and stir well. Pour in the chicken broth and water, and stir well.
5. Season the stew with salt, pepper, and pimenton. Stir well.
6. Bring the stew to a boil, then reduce the heat to low and let it simmer for 1 hour and 30 minutes, or until the pork stomach is tender and the chickpeas are cooked through.
7. Serve hot, with a sprinkle of chopped parsley on top, if desired. Enjoy your Madrid-style callos with some crusty bread!

Huevos a la flamenca

Huevos a la flamenca is a traditional dish from Madrid, Spain that is typically served as a hearty breakfast or brunch dish. The dish is made up of fried eggs served over a bed of sautéed tomato, onion, and pepper. It is a simple yet delicious dish that is perfect for any time of the day.

4 SERVINGS   *20 MINUTES*   *300 KCAL*   *EASY*

INGREDIENTS

- 4 large eggs
- 1 onion, thinly sliced
- 1 red pepper, thinly sliced
- 2 cloves of garlic, minced
- 1 large tomato, peeled and chopped
- 1/2 tsp smoked paprika
- Salt and pepper, to taste
- 2 tablespoons of olive oil

DIRECTIONS

1. Begin by heating a large skillet over medium heat. Add the olive oil and diced onions and cook until the onions are translucent, about 5 minutes.
2. Add the diced bell peppers and cook for an additional 5 minutes, or until the peppers are tender.
3. Crack the eggs into the skillet, spacing them evenly apart.
4. Sprinkle the eggs with a pinch of salt and pepper, and add a splash of water to the skillet.
5. Cover the skillet with a lid and cook for about 2-3 minutes, or until the whites of the eggs are set but the yolks are still runny.
6. Remove the skillet from the heat and top the eggs with the diced tomatoes and chopped parsley.
7. Serve immediately, garnished with additional parsley if desired. Enjoy your delicious huevos a la flamenca!

Cochinillo al horno

Cochinillo al horno is a traditional dish from Madrid, Spain, made with a whole roasted suckling pig. The pig is seasoned with salt, pepper, and sometimes herbs, and cooked slowly in a wood-fired oven until the skin is crispy and the meat is tender and juicy. It is typically served with potatoes and a green salad.

4 SERVINGS | **6 HOURS** | **450 KCAL** | **MED**

INGREDIENTS

- 1 whole suckling pig, about 6-8 kg
- Salt and pepper
- Olive oil
- 4-5 cloves of garlic
- Thyme or rosemary (optional)

DIRECTIONS

1. Start by preparing the pig. Clean the pig thoroughly inside and out, and pat it dry with paper towels. Season the pig liberally with salt and pepper, and rub it with a little olive oil. If desired, you can also add some chopped garlic and thyme or rosemary to the seasoning.
2. Let the pig marinate in the refrigerator for at least 4 hours, or overnight if possible. This will help to enhance the flavor and tenderness of the meat.
3. Preheat your oven to 180C (350F).
4. Place the pig in a roasting pan, and roast it in the oven for about 4 hours, or until the skin is golden brown and crispy and the meat is cooked through.
5. To check if the pig is cooked, insert a meat thermometer into the thickest part of the meat. The internal temperature should reach at least 74C (165F).
6. Once the pig is cooked, remove it from the oven and let it rest for about 10-15 minutes before carving.
7. Serve the cochinillo al horno with potatoes and a green salad. Be sure to save the crispy skin for a special treat!

Enjoy your Cochinillo al horno and savor the flavors of Madrid!

CHAPTER 4

MURCIA

Murcia is a region located in the southeast of Spain, known for its rich cultural heritage and delicious cuisine. The region's culinary scene is heavily influenced by its Mediterranean climate and fertile soil, which produce an abundance of fresh fruits and vegetables.

One of the most popular dishes in Murcia is "Caldero Murciano" which is a traditional seafood stew made with a variety of fish, shellfish, and vegetables. The dish is known for its intense flavors and is a must-try for seafood lovers.

Another popular dish is "Fideuá" which is a type of paella made with short, thin noodles instead of rice. It is traditionally served with a variety of seafood, and is a great alternative to traditional paella.

Murcia is also known for its "Arroz a banda" (rice with fish), which is a classic dish made with fish and seafood cooked with rice. This dish is a staple in many seafood restaurants in the region.

The region is also famous for its "Torta de chicharrones" which is a traditional pork dish, made with crispy pork belly, which is slow-cooked until tender and then served on a slice of bread.

Murcia is also known for its "Espinacas con garbanzos" (spinach with chickpeas) which is a traditional dish of spinach and chickpeas that is popular in the region.

Murcia's cuisine is a perfect blend of traditional and modern flavors and ingredients, with a focus on fresh, seasonal ingredients and traditional cooking methods. Whether you're looking for a hearty stew or a refreshing salad, the region has something to offer for everyone's taste. So if you have a chance to visit Murcia, don't miss the opportunity to try some of the delicious local dishes.

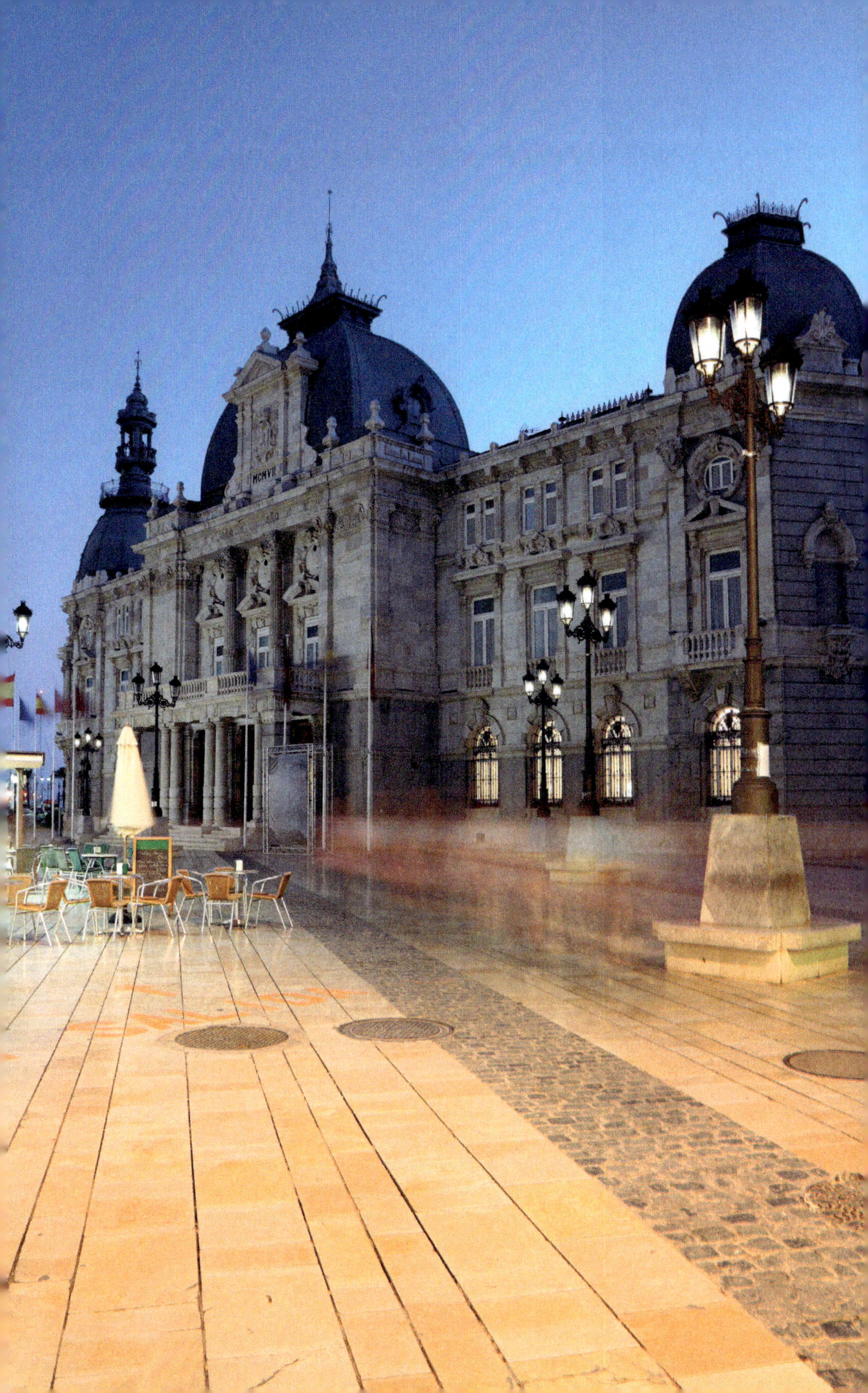
MCMVII

Did you know that...

1. Murcia is known for its traditional dishes that are based on the agricultural products of the region. One of the most famous dishes is "Arroz con costra" which is a type of paella made with eggs, chicken and rabbit and is cooked with saffron and paprika.
2. Murcia is also known for its traditional "Empanadas" which are savory pastries filled with meat, fish or vegetables. They are usually fried and can be found in many local markets and street vendors in the region.
3. The region is also famous for its "Caldero" a traditional seafood stew that is made with fish, seafood, and vegetables. This dish is typically cooked in a clay pot and is served with bread.
4. Murcia is known for its sweet pastries and desserts, such as "Polvorones" which are small, crumbly cakes made with ground almonds, sugar, and cinnamon. They are often served with coffee or tea.
5. The region is also known for its wines, particularly its white wines which are made from the Moscatel grape. These wines are known for their fruity and floral aromas, and are often served as an aperitif or with seafood dishes.
6. Murcia is also famous for its "Jumillana" which is a traditional cured ham, similar to the famous jamón ibérico. This ham is known for its intense flavor and is often served as a tapa.
7. The region is also known for its traditional festivals and celebrations, which feature traditional foods and drinks. For example, the "Fiestas de Moros y Cristianos" festival features dishes such as "Paella Valenciana" and "Arroz con costra"
8. Murcia is a region with a Mediterranean climate, which allows for a wide variety of fruits and vegetables to be grown there, such as oranges, lemons, tomatoes, peppers, and eggplants. These are often used in traditional dishes, adding a unique and refreshing flavor.
9. Murcia cuisine has influences from different cultures, such as the Moors, who occupied the region for centuries, which is why it has a unique blend of flavors and ingredients.
10. Murcia is home to many traditional "Bars" where you can find traditional dishes and tapas, as well as a wide variety of wines. This is a great way to experience the local flavors and culture of the region.

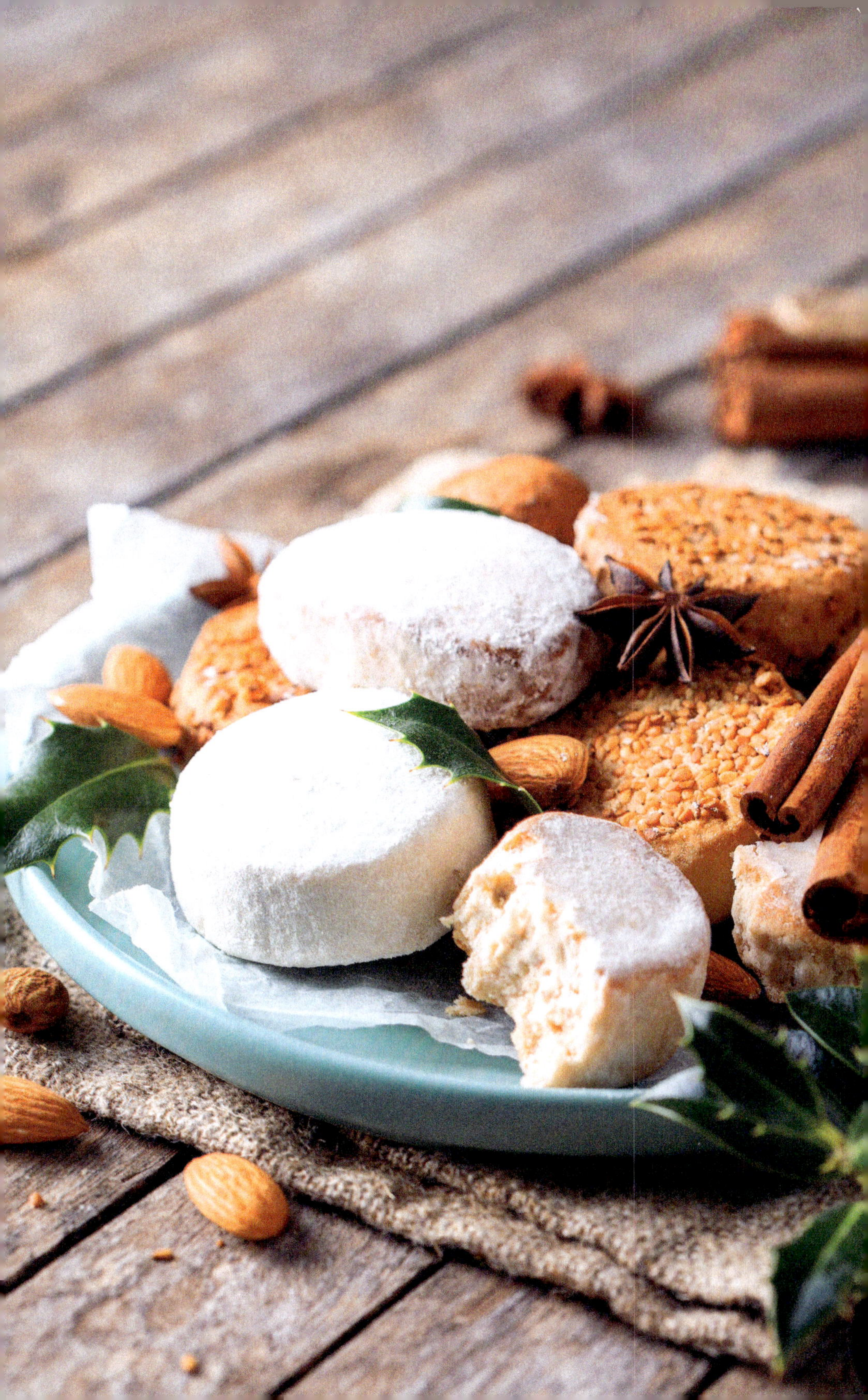

Zarangollo

Zarangollo is a traditional dish from the region of Murcia, Spain. It is a simple and delicious omelette made with zucchini and onions. It is a perfect dish for a light and healthy lunch or dinner.

2 SERVINGS | **20 MINUTES** | **200 KCAL** | **EASY**

INGREDIENTS

- 2 medium zucchinis, grated
- 1 medium onion, finely chopped
- 4 eggs
- 2 tablespoons of olive oil
- Salt and pepper to taste

DIRECTIONS

1. Heat the olive oil in a pan over medium heat.
2. Add the onion and sauté for about 3 minutes until softened.
3. Add the grated zucchinis and continue sautéing for another 5 minutes.
4. Beat the eggs in a bowl with salt and pepper.
5. Add the beaten eggs to the pan with the zucchinis and onions.
6. Cook over low heat for about 8 minutes, until the eggs are set and the bottom of the omelette is golden brown.
7. Carefully flip the omelette and cook for another 2 minutes on the other side.
8. Serve hot and garnish with chopped parsley or chives if desired.

Enjoy this delicious and traditional dish from the region of Murcia. The combination of zucchinis and onions with eggs creates a unique and flavorful dish that is sure to satisfy any palate. It is a perfect dish to serve with a simple salad or some crusty bread. So, next time you want a light and healthy dish for lunch or dinner, give Zarangollo di Murcia a try!

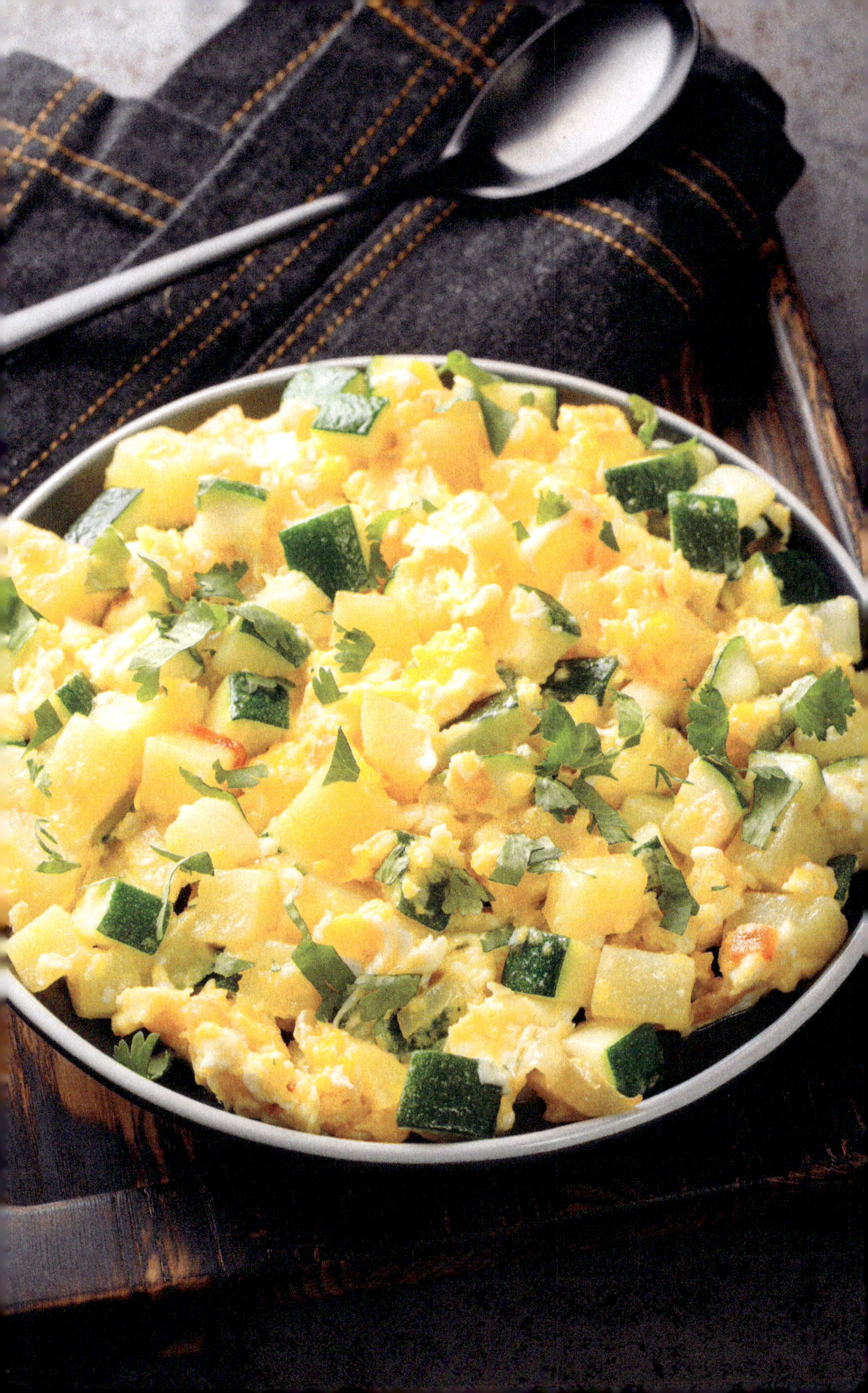

Olla murciana

Olla Murciana is a traditional stew from the region of Murcia in Spain. It's a hearty and comforting dish, typically made with a combination of meats, vegetables, and legumes. It's a popular dish among the locals and is often served as a main course for lunch or dinner.

4 SERVINGS • 90 MINUTES • 600 KCAL • MED

INGREDIENTS

- 2 pounds pork shoulder, cut into cubes
- 1 pound beef, cut into cubes
- 1 pound chorizo, cut into slices
- 1 pound morcilla (blood sausage), cut into slices
- 1 onion, diced
- 2 cloves of garlic, minced
- 1 cup of chickpeas, pre-soaked
- 1 cup of white beans, pre-soaked
- 1 cup of green beans, trimmed and cut into 2-inch pieces
- 2 cups of diced potatoes
- 2 cups of diced carrots
- 2 cups of diced turnips
- 2 cups of diced tomatoes
- 2 cups of chicken or beef broth
- 1 cup of white wine
- Salt and pepper to taste
- Olive oil

DIRECTIONS

1. In a large pot or Dutch oven, heat some olive oil over medium-high heat. Add the pork and beef, and brown them on all sides. Remove the meats from the pot and set them aside.
2. In the same pot, add more oil if needed and sauté the chorizo, morcilla, onion, and garlic until the onion is translucent.
3. Add the meats back into the pot, along with the chickpeas, white beans, green beans, potatoes, carrots, turnips, and diced tomatoes. Pour in the chicken or beef broth and white wine.
4. Season with salt and pepper to taste, and bring the stew to a boil.
5. Reduce the heat to low and let it simmer for about 1 hour, or until the meats and vegetables are tender.
6. Taste and adjust seasoning as needed. Serve hot, with some crusty bread on the side.

This traditional stew from Murcia is a hearty and comforting dish that is perfect for a cold winter evening. The combination of meats, vegetables, and legumes creates a rich and flavorful broth that is sure to warm you up from the inside out. Enjoy with a glass of wine and some crusty bread to soak up all the delicious juices.

Huevos rotos con alcachofas

Huevos rotos con alcachofas di Murcia is a simple yet delicious dish that is popular in the region of Murcia, Spain. It is a variation of the traditional huevos rotos, which is a dish of fried eggs served over a bed of potatoes. The addition of artichokes, which are abundant in the region, gives this dish a unique and delicious flavor.

2 SERVINGS **20 MINUTES** **300 KCAL** **EASY**

INGREDIENTS

- 4 large eggs
- 4 artichokes
- 4 tbsp olive oil
- Salt and pepper to taste
- 2 cloves of garlic

DIRECTIONS

1. Start by preparing the ingredients. Slice the onion and garlic thinly and set aside. Cut the artichokes into thin wedges and set aside. Cut the ham into small cubes and set aside.
2. Heat a large skillet over medium heat and add olive oil. Once hot, add the sliced onions and garlic and sauté until softened and lightly golden.
3. Add the artichoke wedges and ham cubes to the skillet and sauté until the artichokes are tender, about 5-7 minutes.
4. Crack the eggs into the skillet, making sure to spread them out evenly. Season with salt and pepper.
5. Use a spatula to gently stir the eggs and vegetables together, until the eggs are cooked to your liking.
6. Once the eggs are cooked to your liking, remove the skillet from heat and sprinkle chopped parsley over the top. Serve immediately and enjoy with crusty bread for dipping into the delicious sauce.

Almejas a la marinera

The Caldero del Mar Menor is a traditional fish stew from the Murcian region of Spain, specifically from the area around the Mar Menor, a large saltwater lagoon. The dish is made with a variety of fish and seafood, and is typically served with bread on the side. The dish is believed to have originated as a way for local fishermen to use up the catch of the day, and is now considered a staple of Murcian cuisine.

4 SERVINGS   **60 MINUTES**   **300 KCAL**   **MED**

INGREDIENTS

- 1.5 lbs of mixed fish (such as hake, red snapper, squid, and shrimp)
- 3 cloves of garlic, minced
- 1 onion, finely chopped
- 1 red bell pepper, finely chopped
- 1 green bell pepper, finely chopped
- 2 tomatoes, finely chopped
- 1 cup white wine
- 2 cups fish stock
- 1 cup olive oil
- Salt and pepper, to taste
- Lemon wedges, for serving

DIRECTIONS

1. Begin by preparing the fish and shellfish. Clean and devein the shrimp and cut the squid into small rings. Clean and scale the fish, then cut into bite-sized pieces.
2. In a large paella pan or wide, shallow pot, heat the olive oil over medium-high heat. Add the onion and sauté until it becomes translucent.
3. Add the garlic and sauté for another minute.
4. Add the tomato paste and stir to combine. Cook for a couple of minutes, until the tomato paste has darkened in color.
5. Add the saffron and paprika to the pan, stirring for a few seconds until fragrant.
6. Add the short-grain rice and stir to coat it in the tomato mixture.
7. Add the fish stock and bring the mixture to a boil.
8. Reduce the heat to medium-low, and add the fish and shellfish.
9. Allow the mixture to simmer for around 18-20 minutes, or until the rice is cooked through and the liquid has been absorbed.
10. Once the rice is cooked, remove from heat and let rest for a few minutes before serving.
11. Garnish with fresh chopped parsley, and serve with lemon wedges on the side.

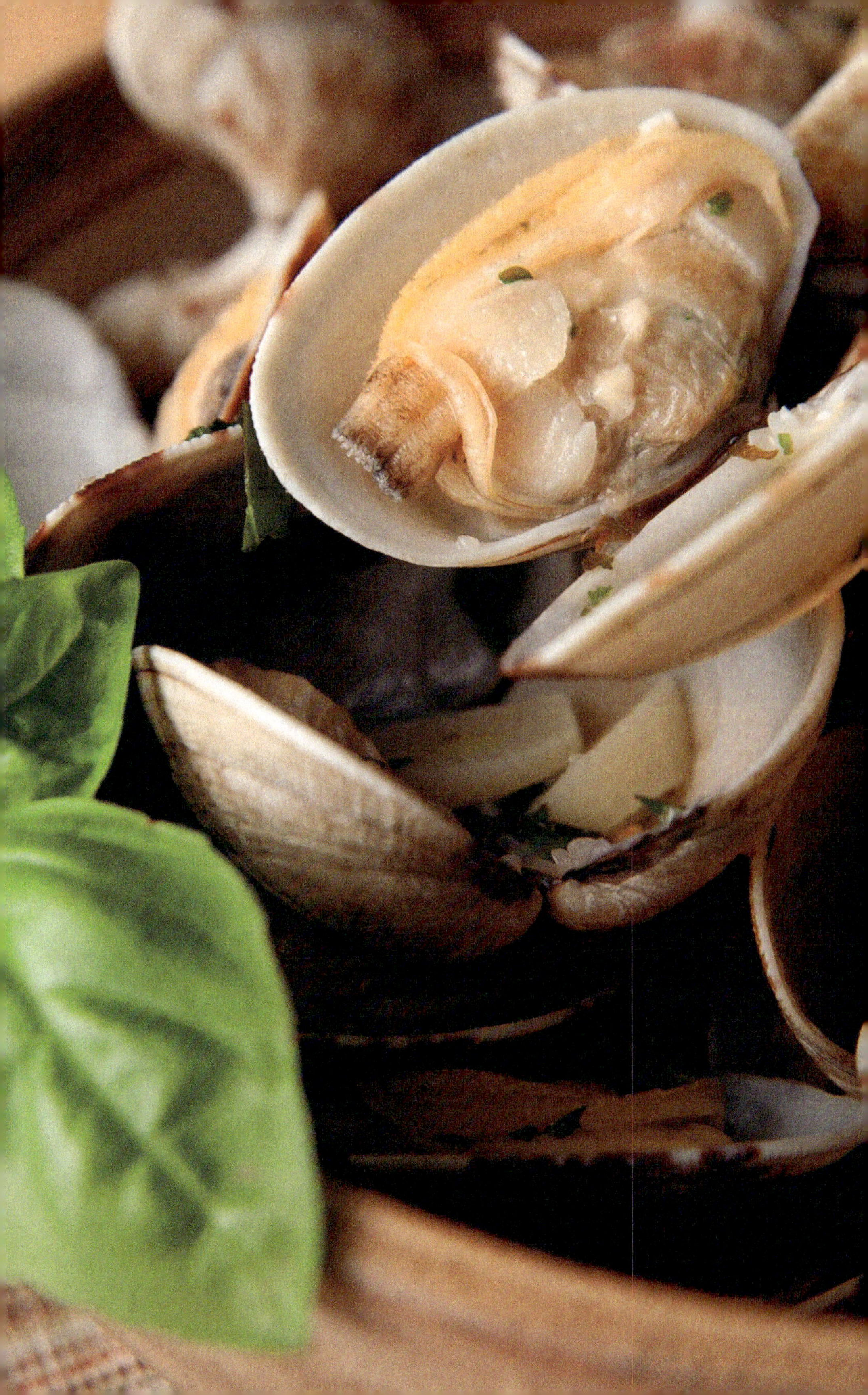

Caldero del Mar Menor

The Caldero del Mar Menor is a traditional fish stew from the Murcian region of Spain, specifically from the area around the Mar Menor, a large saltwater lagoon. The dish is made with a variety of fish and seafood, and is typically served with bread on the side. The dish is believed to have originated as a way for local fishermen to use up the catch of the day, and is now considered a staple of Murcian cuisine.

4 SERVINGS | **60 MINUTES** | **300 KCAL** | **MED**

INGREDIENTS

- 1.5 lbs of mixed fish (such as hake, red snapper, squid, and shrimp)
- 3 cloves of garlic, minced
- 1 onion, finely chopped
- 1 red bell pepper, finely chopped
- 1 green bell pepper, finely chopped
- 2 tomatoes, finely chopped
- 1 cup white wine
- 2 cups fish stock
- 1 cup olive oil
- Salt and pepper, to taste
- Lemon wedges, for serving

DIRECTIONS

1. Begin by preparing the fish and shellfish. Clean and devein the shrimp and cut the squid into small rings. Clean and scale the fish, then cut into bite-sized pieces.
2. In a large paella pan or wide, shallow pot, heat the olive oil over medium-high heat. Add the onion and sauté until it becomes translucent.
3. Add the garlic and sauté for another minute.
4. Add the tomato paste and stir to combine. Cook for a couple of minutes, until the tomato paste has darkened in color.
5. Add the saffron and paprika to the pan, stirring for a few seconds until fragrant.
6. Add the short-grain rice and stir to coat it in the tomato mixture.
7. Add the fish stock and bring the mixture to a boil.
8. Reduce the heat to medium-low, and add the fish and shellfish.
9. Allow the mixture to simmer for around 18-20 minutes, or until the rice is cooked through and the liquid has been absorbed.
10. Once the rice is cooked, remove from heat and let rest for a few minutes before serving.
11. Garnish with fresh chopped parsley, and serve with lemon wedges on the side.

CHAPTER 5

CATALONIA

Catalonia is a region in northeastern Spain, known for its rich culinary heritage and diverse food culture. The region is home to a wide variety of traditional dishes and modern fusion cuisine.

One of the most popular dishes in Catalonia is "Paella", which is a traditional rice dish made with saffron, chicken, rabbit, and vegetables. It's a must-try for those who want to experience the authentic flavors of Catalonia. The dish originates from Valencia, but it's also very popular in Catalonia.

Another popular dish is "Fideuà" which is similar to paella but made with short, thin noodles instead of rice. It's often made with seafood and is a delicious dish that is typically served as a main course.

Catalonia is also known for its "Escalivada" a dish of roasted vegetables, peppers, onions, and eggplant. It's often served as a starter or a side dish and is a great way to experience the region's flavors.

The region is also famous for its "tapas" culture, where you can find a wide variety of traditional and modern dishes such as "patatas bravas" (spicy fried potatoes) and "croquetas" (deep-fried balls of béchamel sauce and various fillings).

Catalonia is also home to a vibrant street food scene, where you can find traditional dishes such as "bocadillos" (sandwiches) and "pan con tomate" (bread with tomato)

Catalonia's cuisine perfectly blends traditional and modern flavors and ingredients, focusing on fresh, seasonal ingredients and traditional cooking methods. Whether you're looking for a hearty stew or a refreshing tapas, the region has something to offer for everyone's taste. So if you can visit Catalonia, don't miss the opportunity to try some of the delicious local dishes.

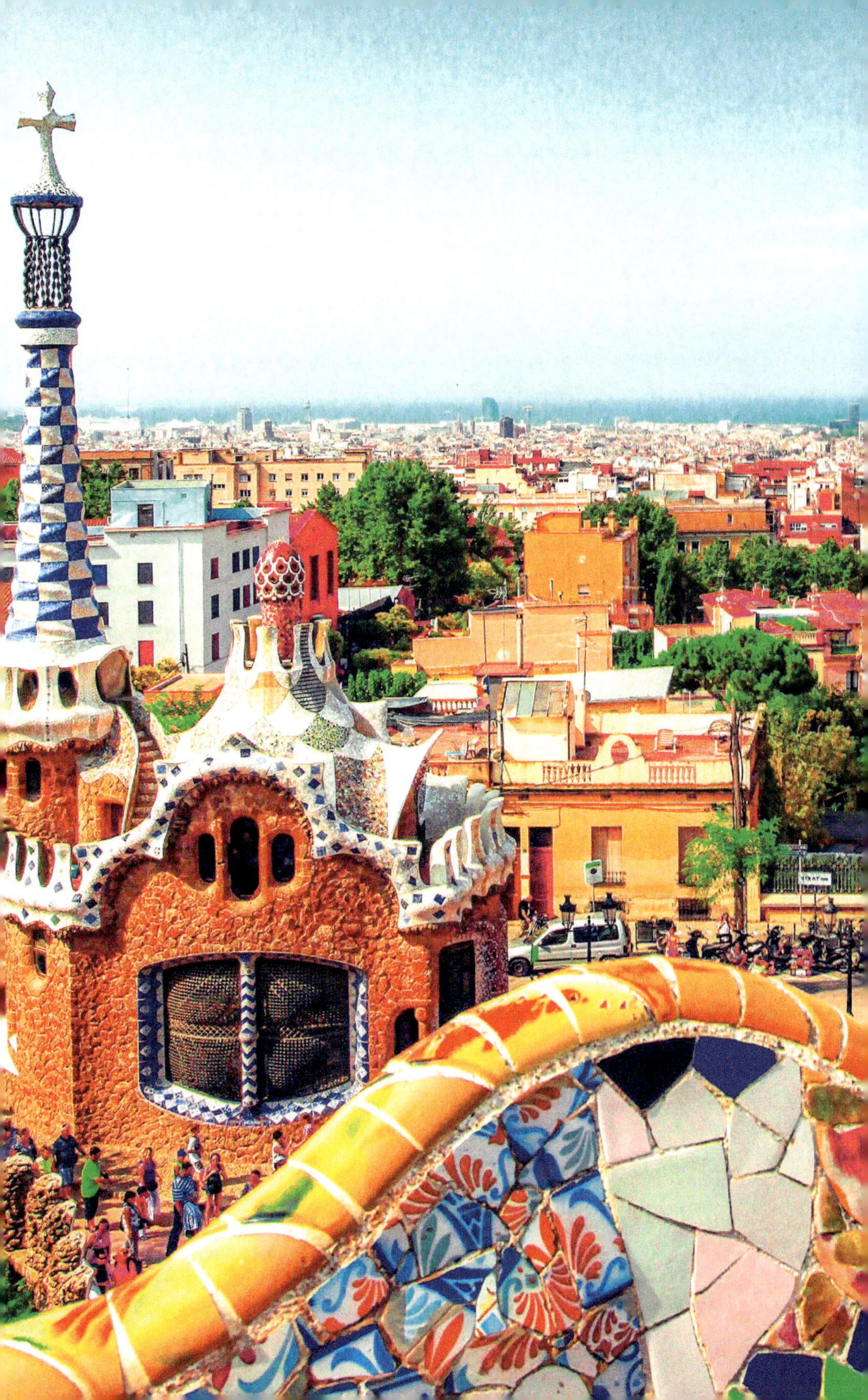

Did you know that...

1. Catalonia is known for its traditional dishes that are based on Mediterranean cuisine. One of the most famous dishes is "Pa amb tomàquet" which is a type of bread rubbed with tomato, olive oil, and salt, usually served as a tapa or a side dish.
2. Catalonia is also known for its traditional "Empanadas" which are savory pastries filled with meat, fish, or vegetables. They are usually fried and can be found in many local markets and street vendors in the region.
3. The region is also famous for its "Suquet de Peix" a traditional fish stew that is made with fish, seafood, and vegetables. This dish is typically cooked in a clay pot and is served with bread.
4. Catalonia is known for its sweet pastries and desserts, such as "Crema Catalana" which is a type of custard made with egg yolks, sugar, and cream and traditionally served on Saint Joseph's Day.
5. The region is also known for its wines, particularly its sparkling wines which are made in the Penedès region. Cava, a sparkling wine made in the traditional method, is considered the most famous and has a Denomination of Origin.
6. Catalonia is also famous for its cured meats, particularly "Fuet" which is a thin and dry sausage made with pork and spices and it is often eaten as a tapa.
7. The region is also known for its traditional festivals and celebrations, which feature traditional foods and drinks. For example, the "La Mercè" festival in Barcelona features dishes such as "Pa amb tomàquet" and "Crema Catalana".
8. Catalonia has a long history of preserving food, which is why it is famous for its charcuterie and pickled vegetables. These traditional techniques are still used today, which give Catalonia's cuisine a unique and intense flavor.
9. Catalonia cuisine has influences from different cultures, such as the French and Italian, which can be seen in dishes like "Butifarra" (Catalan sausage) and "Escudella" (Catalan stew)
10. Catalonia is home to many restaurants, including some of the most famous Michelin-starred restaurants in Spain, and also is known for its traditional "Casas de comidas" (eating houses) where you can find traditional dishes and tapas, as well as a wide variety of wines.

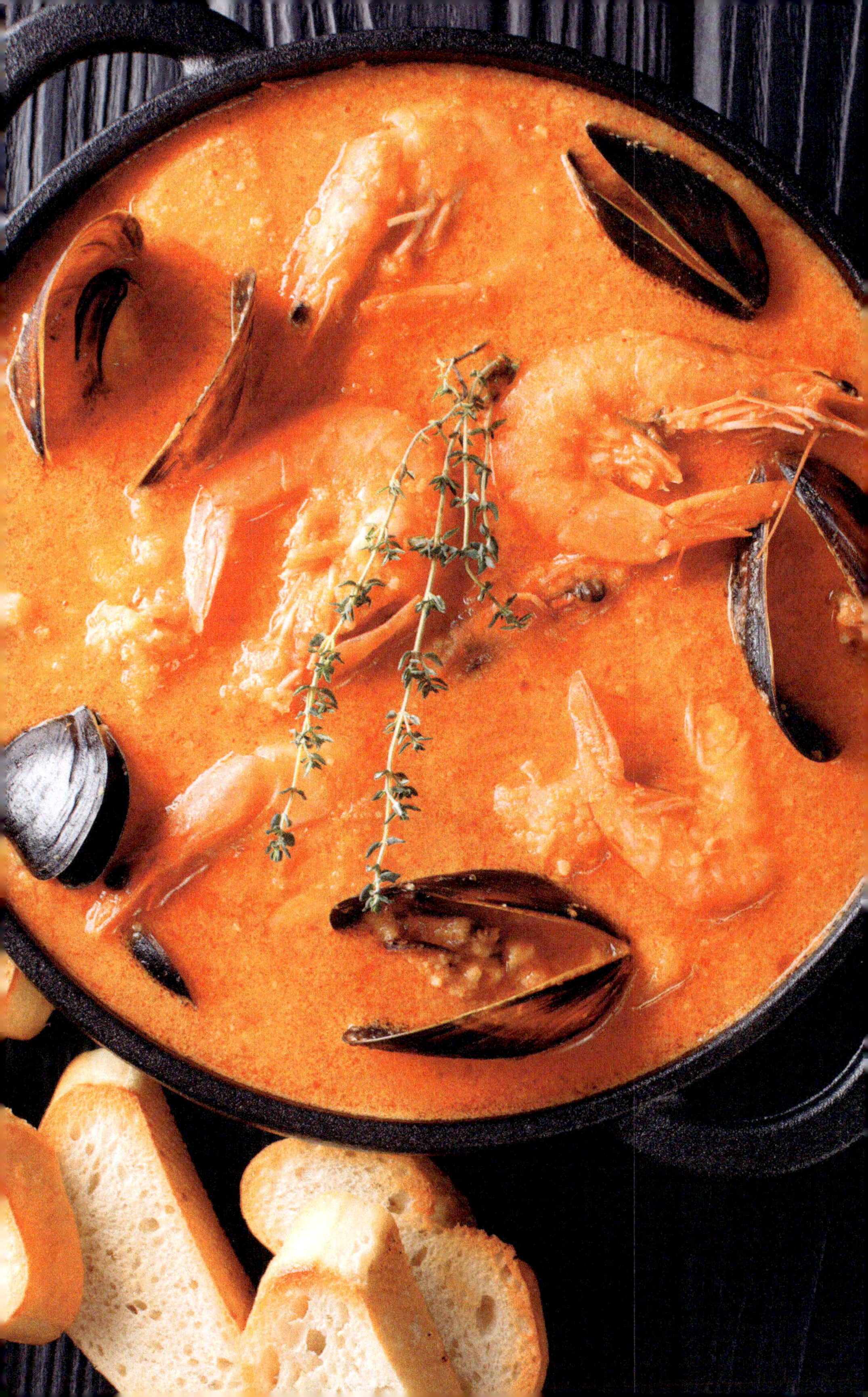

Canelones

Canelones is a traditional dish from Catalonia, Spain, that features large pasta tubes filled with meat and vegetables, then baked in a rich tomato sauce. This dish is a staple in Catalonia and is often served as a main course, it is a hearty and comforting dish that is perfect for cold winter days.

4 SERVINGS **60 MINUTES** **400 KCAL** **MED**

INGREDIENTS

- 12 canelones pasta tubes
- 1/2 lb ground beef
- 1/2 cup chopped onion
- 1/2 cup chopped carrots
- 1/2 cup chopped zucchini
- 2 cloves of garlic, minced
- 2 cups of tomato sauce
- 1 cup of heavy cream
- 1/2 cup of grated parmesan cheese
- Salt and pepper to taste

DIRECTIONS

1. Preheat the oven to 375 degrees F (190 degrees C).
2. Cook the canelones pasta tubes in a large pot of boiling water, following the package instructions. Once cooked, drain and set aside.
3. In a large skillet, brown the ground beef over medium heat. Once browned, add the onions, carrots, zucchini, and garlic. Cook until the vegetables are tender.
4. Add the tomato sauce, cream, and parmesan cheese to the skillet and stir until well combined. Season with salt and pepper to taste.
5. Take a canelone pasta tube and spoon about 2 tablespoons of the meat mixture into it. Roll the pasta tube up to enclose the filling. Repeat with the remaining canelones and meat mixture.
6. Arrange the canelones in a baking dish and pour the remaining tomato sauce over them.
7. Bake in the preheated oven for 25-30 minutes or until the canelones are heated through and the top is golden brown.
8. Serve hot and enjoy the comforting and delicious Catalonia Canelones!

Canelones is a dish that is perfect for a family dinner, it's comforting and hearty and it has a perfect balance of flavors. This dish can also be a great option for entertaining as it can be prepared in advance and reheated before serving.

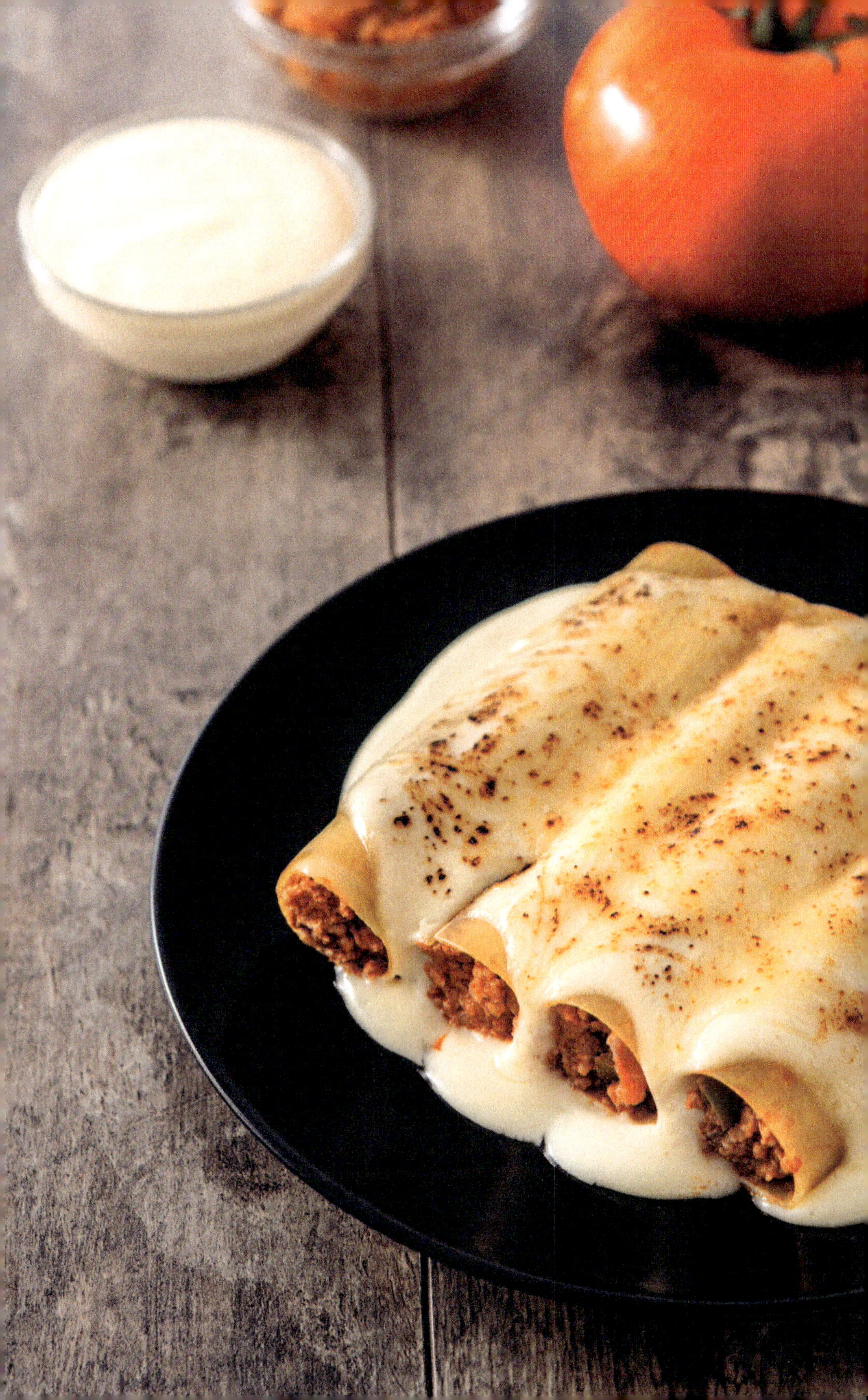

Pulpo a la gallega

"Pulpo a la gallega" or "Galician-style Octopus" is a traditional dish from the Galicia region of Spain. The dish is made by boiling octopus with paprika, olive oil, and salt, and then serving it with boiled potatoes. It is a simple and delicious dish that is often served at festivals and special occasions.

4 SERVINGS   60 MINUTES   300 KCAL   EASY

INGREDIENTS

- 1 lb of octopus
- 1 lb of potatoes
- 1/4 cup of olive oil
- 1 tbsp of paprika
- Salt, to taste

DIRECTIONS

1. Start by cleaning the octopus. Remove the eyes and the beak, and cut the tentacles in bite-sized pieces. Rinse the octopus thoroughly and set it aside.
2. Peel and slice the potatoes into 1/2-inch thick slices.
3. Bring enough water to cover the octopus to a boil in a large pot. Once it reaches a rolling boil, add the octopus and let it cook for about 30 minutes or until it becomes tender.
4. Remove the octopus from the pot and set it aside to cool.
5. In the same pot, add the potatoes and enough water to cover them. Bring the potatoes to a boil and let them cook for about 15 minutes or until they are tender.
6. While the potatoes are cooking, heat the olive oil in a large skillet over medium heat. Once the oil is hot, add the paprika and stir it around for a minute or two.
7. Add the cooked octopus to the skillet with the oil and paprika and stir it around to coat the octopus with the oil. Cook the octopus for a couple of minutes or until it is heated through.
8. Drain the cooked potatoes and add them to the skillet with the octopus. Stir everything together and cook for a few more minutes or until the potatoes are heated through.
9. Season the octopus and potatoes with salt to taste.

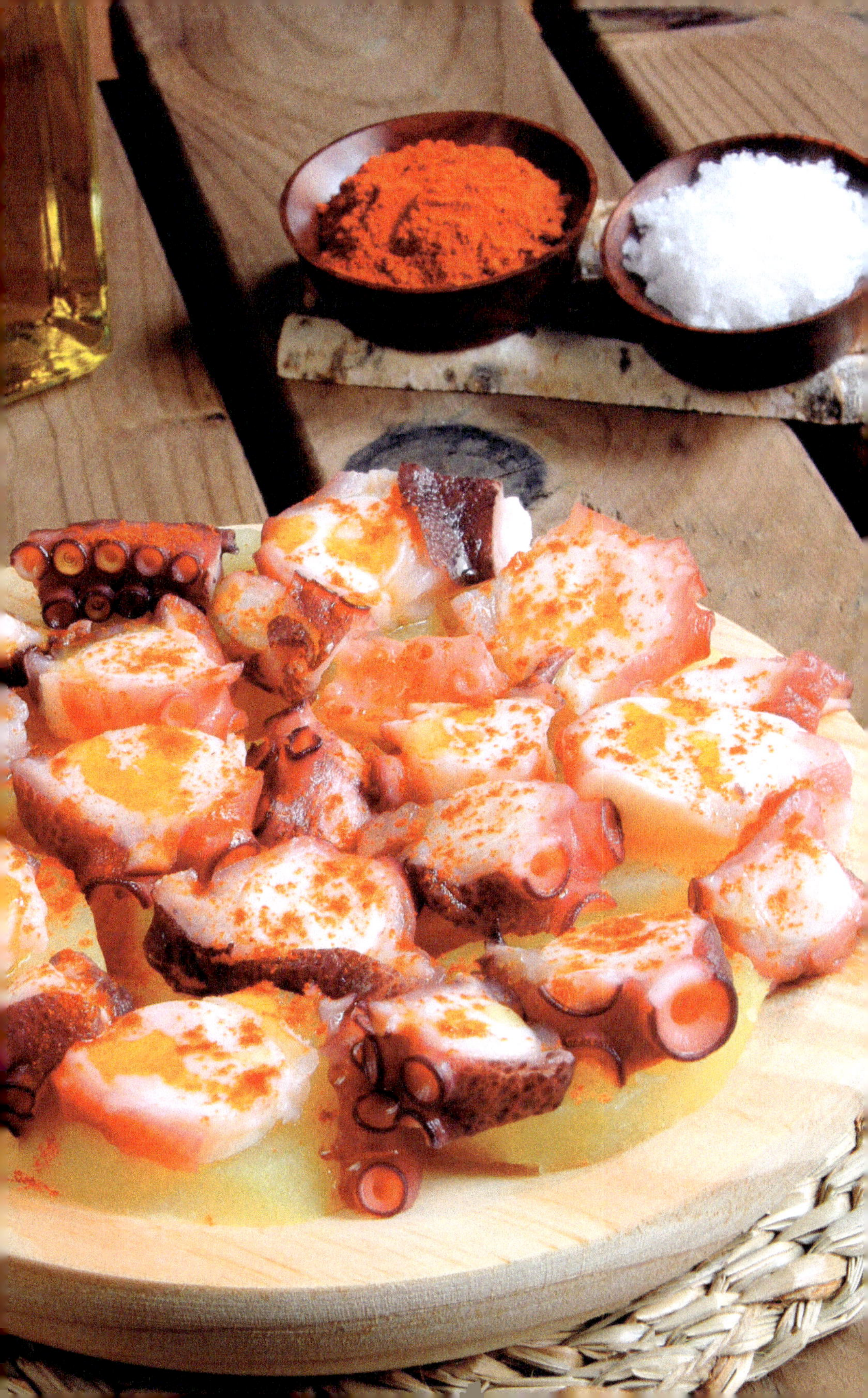

Caldereta de pescado

Caldereta de Pescado is a traditional fish stew that originated in the coastal regions of Spain, particularly in the Mediterranean. This hearty stew is made with a variety of fish, such as hake, cod, or monkfish, and is simmered with potatoes, tomatoes, onions, and peppers in a rich tomato-based broth. The dish is typically flavored with saffron, bay leaves, and paprika, and is finished with a sprinkle of parsley. Caldereta de Pescado is a staple dish in many Spanish households and is often served as a main course with crusty bread to soak up the flavorful broth.

4 SERVINGS | **90 MINUTES** | **600 KCAL** | **MED**

INGREDIENTS

- 1.5 kg of mixed fish (hake, cod, monkfish, etc.)
- 3 potatoes, peeled and diced
- 3 tomatoes, peeled and diced
- 1 onion, finely diced
- 2 bell peppers, finely diced
- 4 cloves of garlic, minced
- 2 cups of fish stock
- 1 cup of white wine
- 1 tsp saffron threads
- 2 bay leaves
- 1 tsp paprika
- Salt and pepper, to taste
- 2 tbsp of parsley, finely chopped

Olive oil, for frying

DIRECTIONS

1. Heat a large pot or casserole over medium heat and add enough olive oil to cover the bottom of the pot.
2. Add the diced onion, bell peppers, and garlic to the pot and sauté until softened, about 5 minutes.
3. Add the diced tomatoes, saffron, bay leaves, paprika, and a pinch of salt and pepper to the pot. Cook for another 5 minutes.
4. Add the fish stock and white wine to the pot, bring the mixture to a simmer, and let it cook for 15 minutes.
5. Add the diced potatoes to the pot and let it simmer for another 15 minutes or until the potatoes are cooked through.
6. Add the fish to the pot and let it cook for another 10 minutes or until the fish is cooked through.
7. Season the stew with additional salt and pepper, if needed.
8. Sprinkle chopped parsley on top of the stew and serve hot with crusty bread.

Queso de cabrales

Queso de Cabrales is a semi-hard blue cheese from the Principality of Asturias, located in Northern Spain. The cheese is made from a combination of cow's milk, sheep's milk, and goat's milk, which gives it a unique flavor and texture. It's a traditional and ancient cheese, made in small batches in the mountains using artisanal techniques.

12 SERVINGS **8** MONTHS **400** KCAL HARD

INGREDIENTS

- 2 gallons of cow's milk
- 1 gallon of sheep's milk
- 1 gallon of goat's milk
- Rennet
- Salt
- Penicillium roqueforti spores

DIRECTIONS

1. Start by heating the milk in a large stainless steel pot over medium-low heat.
2. Once the milk reaches a temperature of 86°F, add the rennet and stir gently for about a minute.
3. Cover the pot and let the mixture sit for about 45 minutes, or until the curd is firm.
4. Cut the curd into small cubes and let it sit for an additional 15 minutes.
5. Slowly heat the curd to a temperature of 102°F, while stirring gently.
6. Once the curd reaches the desired temperature, remove it from the heat and drain it through cheesecloth.
7. Once the curd is drained, it's time to add the salt. Add the salt to the curd and knead it well.
8. Place the curd in molds and press it for 24 hours.
9. After 24 hours, remove the cheese from the molds and place it in a cool and humid room for 8-10 months.
10. During the aging process, the cheese will be exposed to Penicillium roqueforti spores.
11. Once the cheese is aged, it's ready to be served

Sopa de ajo

Sopa de ajo, or garlic soup, is a traditional Spanish dish that is particularly popular in the region of Castilla-La Mancha. The soup is made with a base of garlic, bread, and paprika, and is typically served with a poached egg on top. The dish is hearty and comforting, and is often eaten as a starter or a light meal.

4 SERVINGS   **45 MINUTES**   **300 KCAL**   **EASY**

INGREDIENTS

- 8 cloves of garlic, minced
- 4 cups of chicken broth
- 1 cup of water
- 2 cups of day-old bread, cut into small cubes
- 1 tsp of paprika
- Salt and pepper, to taste
- 4 eggs
- Olive oil, for frying
- Fresh parsley, chopped (optional)

DIRECTIONS

1. Start by heating a large pot over medium-high heat. Add the olive oil and butter, and once the butter is melted, add the garlic and sauté for about 2 minutes, or until fragrant.
2. Stir in the bread and cook for about 3 minutes, or until the bread is toasted and crispy.
3. Slowly pour in the chicken broth, stirring constantly to prevent lumps from forming. Bring the soup to a simmer and let it cook for about 10 minutes, or until the bread has completely dissolved.
4. Season the soup with salt and pepper to taste.
5. Crack the eggs into the pot, one at a time, and gently stir them into the soup.
6. Cook the eggs for about 2 minutes or until the whites are set but the yolks are still runny.
7. Ladle the soup into bowls and serve immediately, garnishing with chopped parsley and a drizzle of olive oil, if desired.

CHAPTER 6

DESSERTS

Spain is renowned for its rich and diverse culinary traditions, and its desserts are no exception. From Catalonia's sweet and flaky pastries to the creamy custards of Andalusia, Spanish desserts offer a wide range of flavors and textures that are sure to delight any palate.

One of the most popular Spanish desserts is Flan, a creamy custard that is often flavored with vanilla or caramel. Flan is believed to have originated in ancient Rome and was brought to Spain by the Moors during the Islamic occupation of the Iberian Peninsula. Today, flan is a staple dessert in Spain and can be found in almost every café and restaurant across the country.

Another classic Spanish dessert is Turron, a nougat-like confection made from almonds and honey. Turron is believed to have originated in the town of Jijona in the region of Valencia, where it has been made for centuries. Turron is a traditional Christmas treat in Spain, and it can be found in many varieties, such as soft and hard.

In the Catalonia region, one can find the famous pastry Pastel de Nata, a traditional pastry made of puff pastry and filled with creme patisserie. The Monks created this pastry in the 18th century in the city of Santa Maria de Montserrat. It is considered a staple pastry in Catalonia and can be found in many pastry shops.

Another famous Spanish dessert is the Crema Catalana, a creamy custard that is similar to flan, but it is flavored with lemon or orange peel and cinnamon. This dessert is traditionally served on Saint Joseph's Day, which is celebrated in Catalonia and other parts of Spain.

Spain also has a wide variety of cakes and pastries that are popular throughout the country. Among the most famous of these is the Tarta de Santiago, a traditional almond cake that is said to have originated in the city of Santiago de Compostela.

Overall, Spanish desserts offer diverse flavors and textures that reflect the country's rich culinary traditions and history. Whether you're looking for a sweet and creamy custard or a flaky pastry, there is a Spanish dessert to suit every taste.

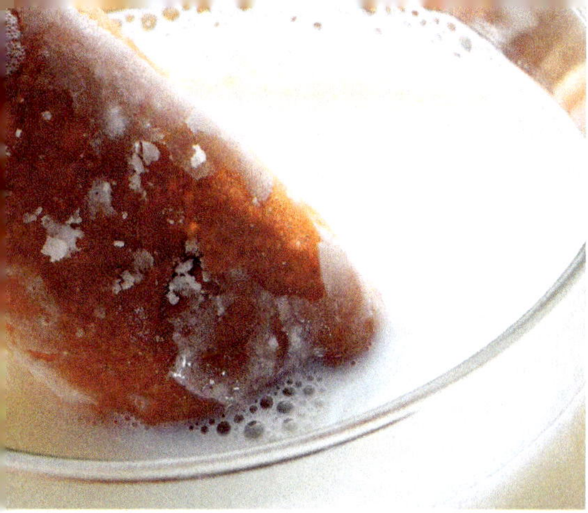
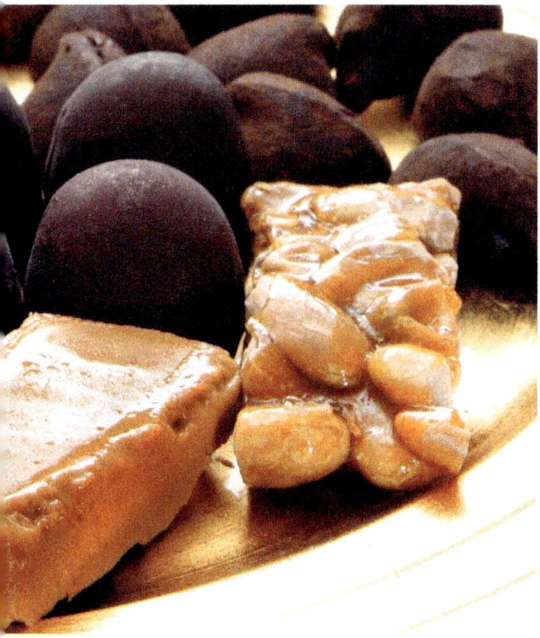
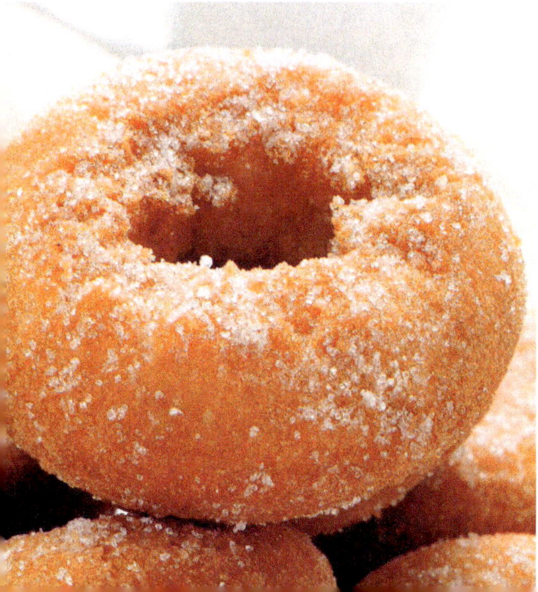
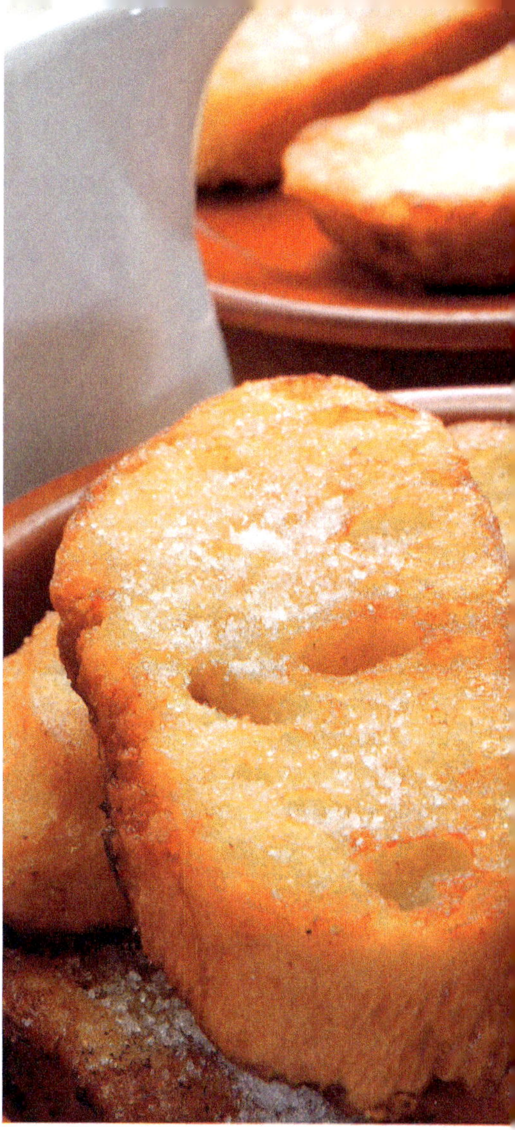
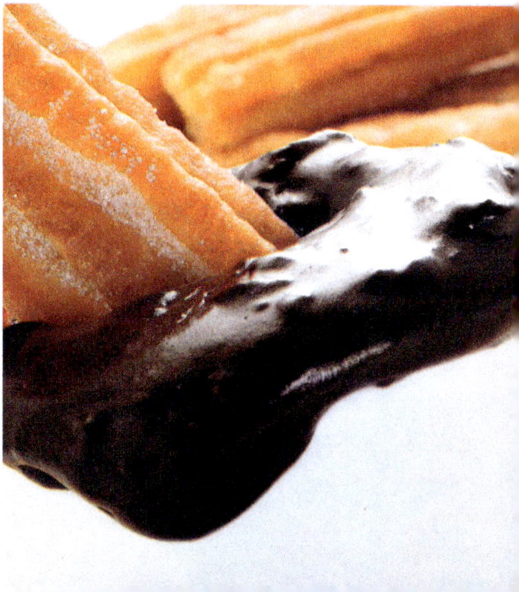

Crema Catalana

Crema catalana is a traditional Spanish dessert from Catalonia that is similar to crème brûlée. It is a rich custard topped with a layer of caramelized sugar. The dish has a long history dating back to the Middle Ages and is traditionally served on Saint Joseph's Day (March 19th).

4 SERVINGS | **55 MINUTES** | **400 KCAL** | **EASY**

INGREDIENTS

- 1 quart heavy cream
- 1 vanilla bean, split and scraped
- 1 cinnamon stick
- 6 large egg yolks
- 1/2 cup granulated sugar
- 1/4 cup cornstarch
- 1/4 cup orange zest
- 1/4 cup lemon zest
- 1/4 cup sugar for caramelizing

DIRECTIONS

1. In a medium saucepan, heat the cream, vanilla bean, and cinnamon stick over medium heat until it just comes to a boil. Remove from heat and let steep for 10 minutes.
2. In a separate bowl, whisk together the egg yolks, granulated sugar, cornstarch, orange zest, and lemon zest until well combined.
3. Slowly pour the hot cream mixture into the egg mixture, whisking constantly to prevent curdling.
4. Pour the mixture back into the saucepan and cook over medium-low heat, stirring constantly, until the mixture thickens, about 10 minutes.
5. Remove the pan from the heat and strain the mixture through a fine-mesh sieve into a large bowl. Discard the solids.
6. Divide the custard mixture evenly among four ramekins. Place the ramekins in a large baking dish and fill the dish with enough hot water to come halfway up the sides of the ramekins.
7. Bake the custards in a preheated 350°F oven until set, about 20 minutes.
8. Remove the ramekins from the baking dish and let cool to room temperature.
9. Once cooled, evenly sprinkle 1 tablespoon of sugar over the top of each custard. Using a kitchen torch, caramelize the sugar until golden brown and bubbly. Let cool for a few minutes before serving.

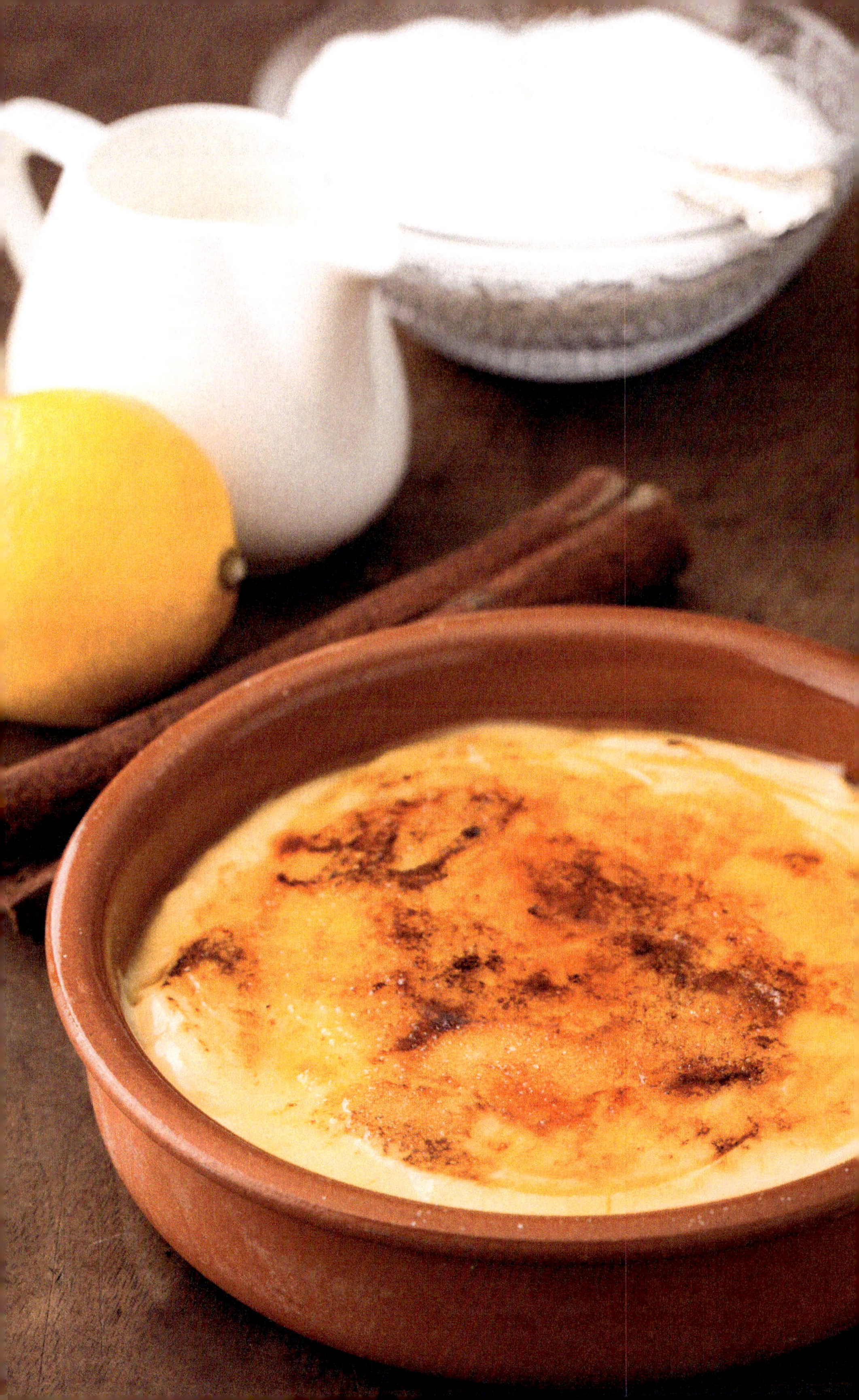

Chocolate and Churros

Chocolate and Churros is a classic Spanish breakfast dish that features crispy, fried dough sticks (churros) that are dipped in a rich, warm chocolate sauce. The dish is said to have originated in Spain during the 16th century, and it is now enjoyed by people all over the world. It's a perfect combination of sweet, salty and crispy textures.

4 SERVINGS | **30 MINUTES** | **400 KCAL** | **MED**

INGREDIENTS

- 2 cups of water
- 1/2 cup of unsalted butter
- 1/2 cup of sugar
- 1 teaspoon of salt
- 1 cup of all-purpose flour
- 3 eggs
- Oil for deep-frying
- 1 cup of heavy cream
- 8 oz of dark chocolate, chopped

DIRECTIONS

1. In a large saucepan, bring the water, butter, sugar, and salt to a boil over medium heat. Once the butter has melted, add the flour and stir until a dough forms.
2. Remove the pan from the heat and let it cool for a few minutes. Once cooled, add the eggs one at a time, stirring until the dough is smooth and shiny.
3. Heat the oil in a deep-fryer or a large pot to 350 degrees F (175 degrees C).
4. Using a pastry bag with a star tip, pipe the dough into the hot oil, making 5-inch long churros. Fry the churros until they are golden brown and crispy, about 3-5 minutes.
5. Remove the churros from the oil and drain them on a plate lined with paper towels.
6. In a separate saucepan, heat the cream over medium heat until it comes to a simmer. Remove from heat and add the chopped chocolate, stirring until the chocolate is melted and the mixture is smooth.
7. Dip the churros into the chocolate sauce and enjoy while they are still warm.

Chocolate and churros is a perfect combination of sweet and salty, with crispy churros and rich chocolate sauce. This dish is perfect for breakfast, brunch, or as dessert. It's a traditional Spanish dish that is enjoyed by people all over the world, and it's a perfect way to start your day or finish a meal.

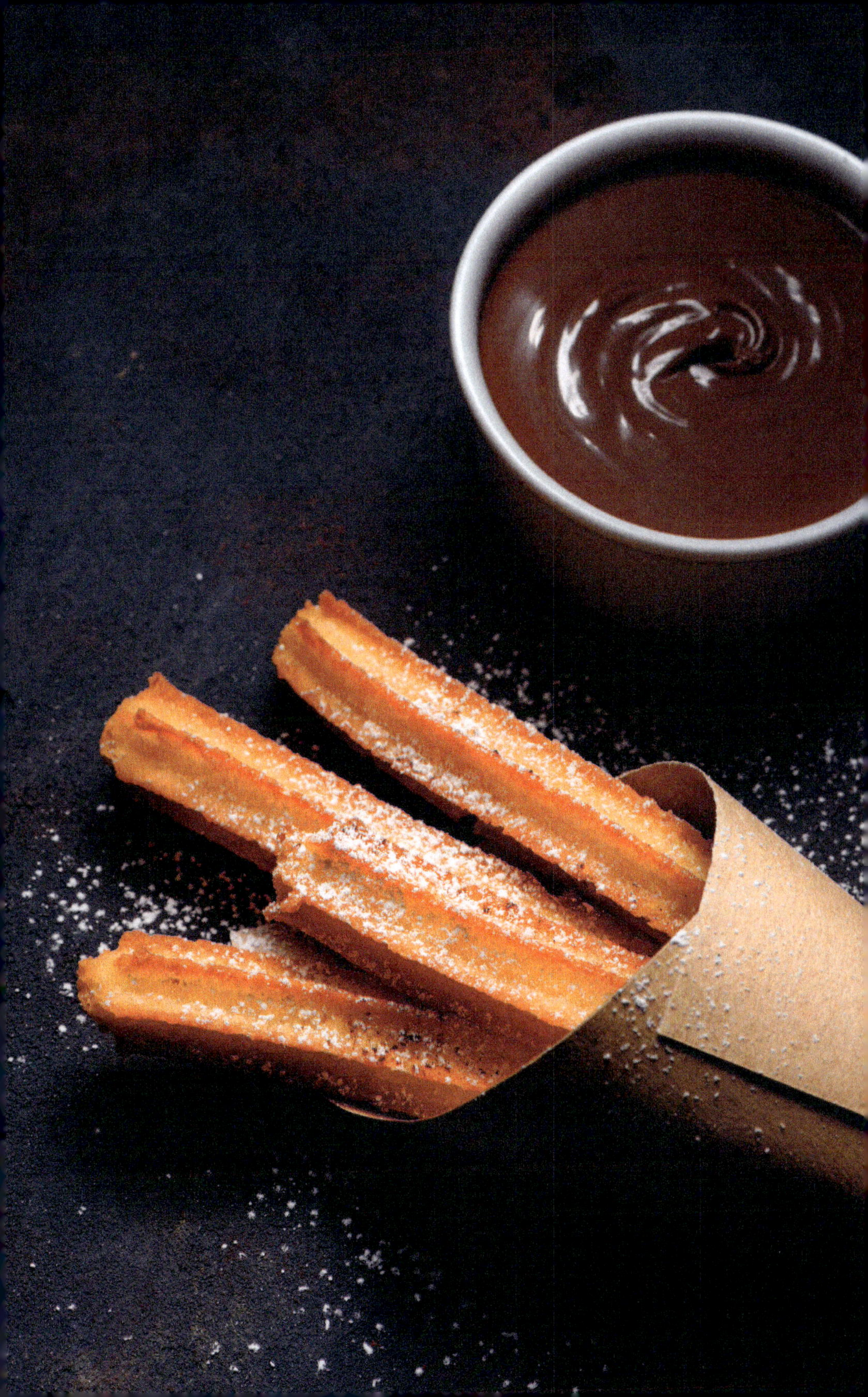

Tarta de Queso

Tarta de Queso is a traditional Spanish cheesecake that is made with a combination of cream cheese, eggs, sugar, and a buttery cookie crust. This dessert is simple, yet delicious and it's a staple in many Spanish households. The dish is believed to have originated in the northern regions of Spain, such as Asturias, Cantabria and the Basque Country, where dairy products are a staple.

8 SERVINGS | **75 MINUTES** | **300 KCAL** | **MED**

INGREDIENTS

- 1 1/2 cups of crushed cookies (such as Maria or Digestive)
- 1/4 cup of unsalted butter, melted
- 1 lb of cream cheese, at room temperature
- 1 cup of sugar
- 3 eggs
- 1 teaspoon of vanilla extract
- Powdered sugar for dusting

DIRECTIONS

1. Preheat the oven to 350 degrees F (175 degrees C). Grease a 9-inch round cake pan.
2. In a medium bowl, combine the crushed cookies and melted butter. Press the mixture into the bottom of the prepared pan.
3. In a separate bowl, beat the cream cheese and sugar until smooth. Beat in the eggs one at a time, then stir in the vanilla extract.
4. Pour the mixture over the crust.
5. Bake in the preheated oven for 45-50 minutes or until the center is almost set.
6. Allow the cheesecake to cool before refrigerating for at least 2 hours.
7. Once chilled, dust with powdered sugar and serve.

Tarta de Queso is a creamy and delicious cheesecake that is perfect for any occasion. It's a classic Spanish dessert that is easy to make and can be enjoyed plain or topped with fresh fruit, or a drizzle of caramel or chocolate sauce. This cheesecake is a great option for entertaining as it can be made ahead of time and chilled until ready to serve.

Leche Frita

Leche Frita is a traditional Spanish dessert that consists of a sweet milk custard that is shaped into squares or balls and then deep-fried until golden brown. The custard is typically flavored with vanilla or lemon zest, and it's often dusted with powdered sugar or cinnamon before serving. The dish is believed to have originated in medieval times as a way to use up surplus milk, and it's a beloved and comforting dessert in Spain.

4 SERVINGS *45 MINUTES* *350 KCAL* *MED*

INGREDIENTS

- 4 cups of milk
- 1/2 cup of sugar
- 1/4 cup of cornstarch
- 1 teaspoon of vanilla extract or grated lemon zest
- Powdered sugar or ground cinnamon for dusting
- Oil for deep-frying

DIRECTIONS

1. In a medium saucepan, combine the milk and sugar and bring to a simmer over medium heat.
2. Mix the cornstarch with a tablespoon of cold milk in a separate bowl to form a paste.
3. Slowly pour the cornstarch mixture into the simmering milk, stirring constantly.
4. Cook for a few minutes, stirring until the mixture thickens.
5. Remove from heat and stir in vanilla extract or lemon zest.
6. Pour the mixture into a greased 9x9 inch square pan and let it cool to room temperature.
7. Once cooled, cut the custard into squares or balls.
8. Heat the oil in a deep-fryer or a large pot to 350 degrees F (175 degrees C).
9. Carefully add the custard squares or balls to the hot oil and fry until they are golden brown and crispy, about 3-5 minutes.
10. Remove the leche frita from the oil and drain them on a plate lined with paper towels.
11. Dust the leche frita with powdered sugar

Tarta de Santiago

Tarta de Santiago is a traditional Spanish almond cake that hails from the city of Santiago de Compostela in Galicia, Spain. The cake is typically made with almonds, sugar and eggs, and it is often decorated with the symbol of the city, the Saint James cross. The cake is said to have originated in the Middle Ages as a way to use up surplus almonds from the local monasteries. Today, it is a beloved and traditional dessert in the region and it's enjoyed by people all over Spain and beyond.

4 SERVINGS *75 MINUTES* *350 KCAL* *MED*

INGREDIENTS

- 1 cup of ground almonds
- 1/2 cup of all-purpose flour
- 1/2 cup of sugar
- 1/2 cup of butter, at room temperature
- 4 eggs
- 1 teaspoon of almond extract
- Powdered sugar for dusting

DIRECTIONS

1. Preheat the oven to 350 degrees F (175 degrees C). Grease a 9-inch round cake pan.
2. In a medium bowl, combine the ground almonds, flour and sugar.
3. In a separate bowl, beat the butter and eggs until light and fluffy. Stir in the almond extract.
4. Gradually add the dry ingredients to the butter mixture and mix until well combined.
5. Pour the batter into the prepared pan and smooth the top.
6. Bake in the preheated oven for 25-30 minutes, or until a toothpick inserted into the center comes out clean.
7. Allow the cake to cool for 10 minutes before removing it from the pan. Let the cake cool completely on a wire rack.
8. Once cooled, dust with powdered sugar and serve

Tarta de Santiago is a traditional Spanish almond cake that is perfect for any occasion. It's a delicious and comforting dessert, the almond flavor is subtle and it's not overly sweet. This cake is easy to make and can be enjoyed plain or topped with fresh fruit, whipped cream or a drizzle of honey. It's a great way to enjoy a piece of Spanish culinary culture and tradition.

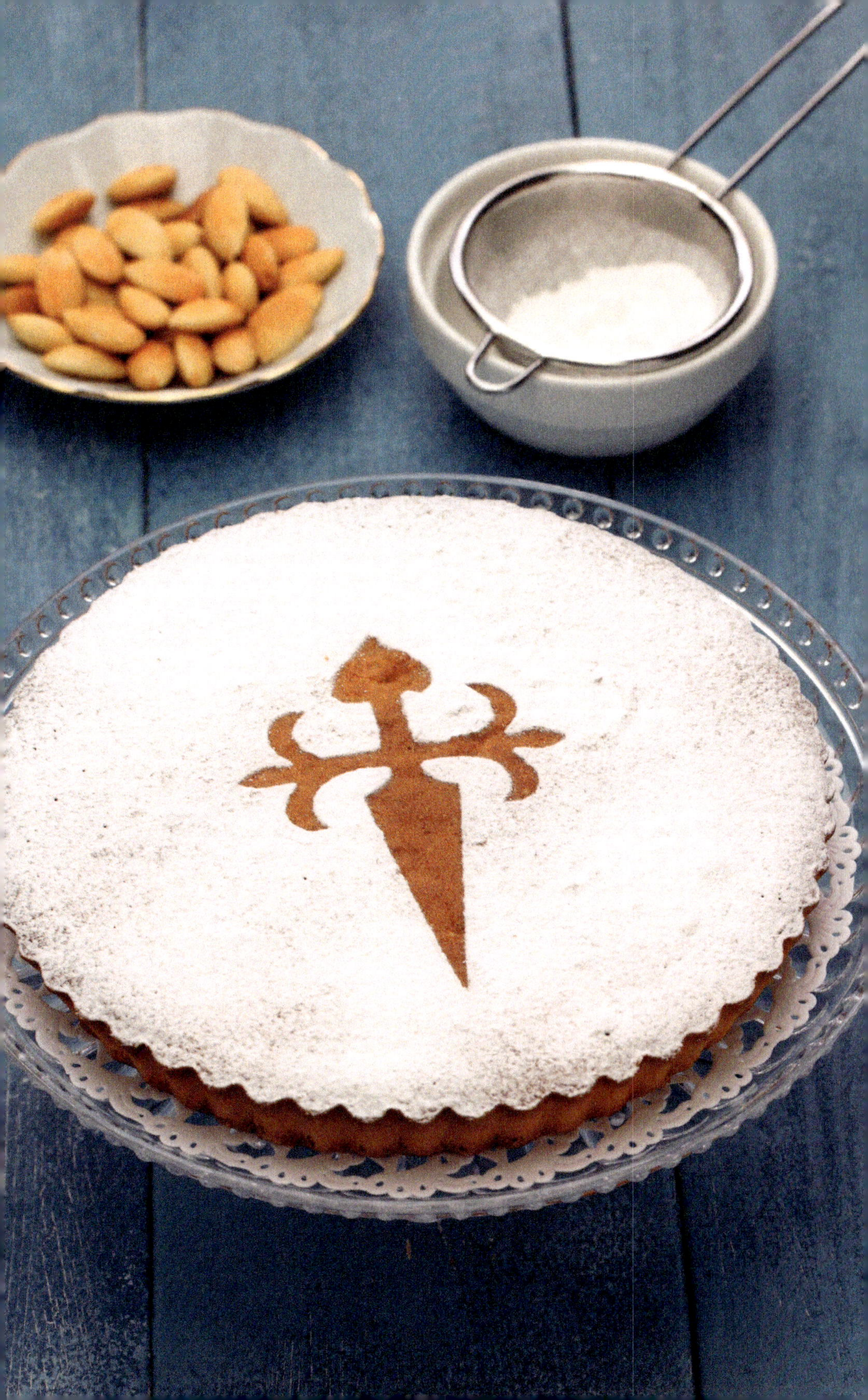

CONCLUSIONS

In conclusion, Spanish cuisine is a melting pot of flavors and influences that have developed over centuries of history. Spanish food celebrates fresh ingredients and bold flavors, from the traditional dishes of paella and tapas to the more modern interpretations of classic recipes. The dishes featured in this book are a small representation of Spain's vast and diverse cuisine. Whether you're a seasoned cook or just starting out, we hope this book has inspired you to create some delicious Spanish dishes in your own kitchen.

One thing that makes Spanish cuisine so unique is the emphasis on using fresh, local ingredients. Whether it's the juicy tomatoes and peppers of Andalusia, the succulent seafood of the coast, or the rich, nutty flavor of Spanish olive oil, the ingredients used in Spanish cooking are of the highest quality. This is why it's essential to use the best ingredients that you can find, whether you're making a simple dish like a tortilla or a more complex dish like paella.

Another thing that separates Spanish cuisine is the focus on communal eating and shared plates. Tapas, pintxos and raciones are all dishes meant to be shared and enjoyed with friends and family. This is a great way to experience a variety of flavors and dishes and also a great way to bond with loved ones over a delicious meal.

This book covers a wide range of dishes from across Spain, each with its unique flavor and history. From the hearty stews of the north to the fresh seafood of the south, there is something for everyone in Spanish cuisine. We hope that you've enjoyed exploring the flavors and traditions of Spain through this book and that you will continue to discover and enjoy Spanish food for years to come.

Printed in Great Britain
by Amazon